MW00900577

From the Gun
to the Pulpit

From the Gun
to the Pulpit

Fr. Drew

Copyright © 2010 by Fr. Andrew C. Smith Jr.

Library of Congress Control Number:		2010915150
ISBN:	Softcover	978-1-4535-9439-1
	Ebook	978-1-4535-9440-7

All rights reserved. No part of this book may be reproduced or transmitted in any form or by any means, electronic or mechanical, including photocopying, recording, or by any information storage and retrieval system, without permission in writing from the copyright owner.

Disclaimer/Note to reader
This is a true account. The incidents portrayed are all based on actual events, but many are composites, the names and certain other identifying characteristics have been changed. The foul language in the book is used because of the nature of the work that I was involved in and isn't meant to offend anyone.

This book was printed in the United States of America.

To order additional copies of this book, contact:
Xlibris Corporation
1-888-795-4274
www.Xlibris.com
Orders@Xlibris.com
88465

Contents

Preface

Beat 631 and units in the sixth district we are getting a call of shots fired at 94th and Parnell. As we arrive on the scene, blood curdling, screams and shouting fill the air. Other officers arrive. We struggle to make our way through the growing crowd. In the middle of the crowd, two young African-American men are lying in a pool of blood. The ambulance arrives to carry the young men to the hospital. I think to myself, "What in the world have I gotten myself into?"

These young men are lucky. They survive the shooting. Nevertheless, in the days and years to come thousands of calls of shots fired come in. The result is the death of many young African-American men who would fail to reach their full potential in life. These young men could have been my classmates. They could have played ball with me, and in a sense they were me—a young African-American male growing up on the south side of Chicago. Over the course of the next ten years I saw this story play itself out over and over again.

The goal of this book is to chronicle my transformation from a young kid just graduating from college into an animal on the streets of Chicago and then into a man of God. It is only through the power of the Holy Spirit that I was able to respond to my call to the priesthood.

When I first joined the Chicago Police Department I was initially terrified of the streets. As a kid growing up on the south side of Chicago I was often exposed to violence and social disorder. However, being a police officer meant that I had to walk into situations on the streets that tested my spirituality and my sanity. I needed to cope, therefore I turned to my friend-Jack Daniels. Ultimately, I was seduced by the allure of danger, women and liquor.

My goal in this book is to present myself not as a saint or role model. But my goal is to hold up my life up as a living witness to the power of the Holy Spirit.

Part I

Surviving

Chapter 1

Training Days

First Roll-Call

Joining the Chicago Police Department was a way for me to serve the people. I looked forward to serving the City of Chicago as a police officer. I received the letter telling me that I was hired and the instruction to report to the training academy on 30JAN91. On my first day at the training academy one of the instructors said, "Congratulations, you are a part of the biggest, toughest, most sophisticated gang in the city of Chicago." One of the recruits replied, "Now that's what I'm talking about." That recruit was me. I liked the idea of helping the community. However, I liked the power of the gun and the badge. I was torn by both urges-to serve the Lord and to be reckless. These two urges are reoccurring themes in my life. Human beings are complex people, but we are called to live a life of freedom by adhering to God's word.

I was beginning my second month in the training academy when the Rodney King incident occurred. Rodney King was severely beaten by several police officers and I remember some of the instructors saying why the officers were justified in using the force that they did. They had me so fired up that I was ready to beat the hell out of Rodney King. I was trained that the goal was to go home at night. One of the instructors said, "As a police officer you will learn how to become a trained observer." I came to understand that when you're on the streets there are all sorts of things happening right before your very eyes and you have to be aware of your surroundings at all times.

The instructors told us that you have to be careful on the street because "the bad guys" are very crafty. "The bad guys" are the offenders who have their own set of rules. "The bad guys" work 24-7 and they will do whatever it takes to survive on the streets. The instructors claim the video of the Rodney King beating is deceiving because he still had the ability to harm the officers because he wasn't under control. I didn't believe them at all, but as a ten-year veteran of the Chicago Police Department I understand that emotions can run high and as a result excessive force is sometimes used. It's not right, but it happens.

I enjoyed my time in the training academy. I really enjoyed the stories that some of the instructors would share with us. I found some of them to be unbelievable, but when I finally hit the streets I knew that they were real!

During the last few weeks in the training academy we were going through scenarios of actual police shootings. I began to laugh as one of the officers started to re-enact a scene of an offender who robbed a bank, shot a few people and then barricaded himself and threatened to commit suicide. I wasn't laughing because people were actually killed in an incident like this. I was laughing because he was so good at it, and it seemed like it was something from one of those old James Cagney movies, and the one that comes to my mind is *Angels with Dirty faces* because the officer was so intense. He could have been an actor himself. I had never experienced anything like that before, and so on one level I thought it was a joke. When the officers were done, they called me up for the first simulation exercise that went like this: I was responding to a call of a burglary in progress. I went to the scene and searched the house and all of a sudden "the bad guy" comes up from behind me and shoots me in the head. The training officer looked at me and said, "This shit is not so funny now is it Smith?" The instructor looked at the class and said, "This job can get you killed!" The entire class sat watching in silence. I looked at their faces and they seemed as if they were more shaken up than I was. Embarrassed, head down, walking back to my seat, I didn't laugh during class anymore, even if something was funny.

The day finally came when I graduated from the training academy. My mother and grandmother came up for the ceremony. My father would have been there but he was at work, after all he had to support his family and he had just dropped a lot of money on the equipment I needed for my job as a police officer. I looked around at the friends that I had made while undergoing training. I could feel a sense of relief that our time in the training academy had come to an end, but there was also a feeling of nervous energy as we were heading into our field-training units. Field training was eight weeks with a field-training officer (FTO) in one of the twenty-five police districts within the City of Chicago. Each police district is unique because each district has its own personality. Some districts have excellent restaurants, stores, and museums and low crime. Other districts have abandoned buildings, mom and pop stores, and high crime.

My first assignment as a police officer was in the sixth district (Gresham). At that time the sixth district was located at 85th and Green. Gresham is one of 77 official community areas on the south side of Chicago. Gresham is a nice middle class African-American community. In Gresham there are nice homes and manicured lawns, but it also has its share of apartment buildings that aren't well maintained. In police terms, it was a pretty fast district because a great deal of calls regarding violent crimes would come in.

I was assigned to the third watch. The hours for the third watch were 3:00PM until 11:00PM and 4:00PM until midnight. When I walked in the station for my first day of training some big giant looking policeman said, "I smell fresh leather goods." He was referring to my gunbelt and holster, which I bought to begin training at the police academy. Let's just call him Monster. Monster stood about 6 feet 3 and weighed about 300 pounds. He was a big sloppy looking guy. His uniform was always dirty and unkempt. He had a scruffy beard and a boisterous attitude and he was a very strong and aggressive police officer. He wore a lot of cologne and one could smell him a mile away. Monster worked the job like he ate his food…extremely fast. I don't even think he took the time to chew at all. He just gulped then he swallowed.

Monster shouted, "Yo rookie the watch commander's office is to the left and around the corner." When I followed his directions I was looking at the women's locker room. A beautiful officer by the name of lovely Laura looked at me and said, "What the hell are you looking at? You are the lowest thing in this building so keep moving." I told her that I was looking for the watch commander's office and she said, "Keep looking." I was thinking to myself, there is a great deal of hostility here.

The building was so small that I eventually found my way to the watch commander's office and the Captain of the third watch was there with the Field Lieutenant. They looked at me and laughed. The Captain said, "You must be Officer Smith." I said, "Yes sir." Captain Burnside said, "Welcome to the sixth district. I am the watch commander. Your field-training officer is Ole Smooth. He is a good officer and he will teach you the ropes." All of a sudden the Lieutenant walks out of the office and hollers, "Roll-call yall." The Captain said, "Follow me Smith." He led me to the roll-call room and shouted, "Fall in." Captain Burnside had all the officers line up for inspection. He walked down the line making sure that we were dressed properly and had all of our equipment. When he approached Monster, he said, "Tuck in your shirt, and where is your vest?" Monster tucked in his shirt and said that his vest was in his locker. Captain Burnside said, "Make sure you put it on before you hit the street." Monster did not like to wear his vest.

Ole Smooth

After roll call my field-training officer came and introduced himself to me. I like to call him Ole Smooth because he was laidback, but he didn't take any shit! He looked down at my feet and saw my shoes. I was wearing the patent leather shoes I wore when I was in the training academy. Ole Smooth said, "Where in the fuck do you think you are going with those cheap ass shoes on?" He got on the radio and notified the dispatcher that we were going to do an equipment adjustment. An equipment adjustment has to do with the things an officer needs for duty such as a uniform, radio, vehicle, etc. that needs adjusting. He took me to Sears and told me to buy some boots. Ole Smooth said, "The only time I want to see you with those patent leather shoes on is at the St. Jude parade." St. Jude is the annual parade in memory of police officers killed in the line of duty. I laughed, but Ole Smooth looked at me and said, "I'm serious! You are going to be running through alleys and yards filled with broken glass. What happens if a nail goes through those play shoes you have on?"

When I sat in the squad car anxiously waiting to receive my first call Ole Smooth said, "This job could get you killed. Our motto is safety first. In order for you to have a long career you need to watch out for the three B's. (Broads, Booze, and Bullets) You are just starting so you have to be smart. Remember this; the ink is not even dry on your application yet." Ole Smooth said, "You are closer to the penitentiary now than you have ever been. I didn't fully comprehend what he meant at the time, but in retrospect Ole Smooth was letting me know that it is easy for a police officer to get caught up in all sorts of illegal activity because of the nature of the job and the people that an officer comes into contact with.

A police officer comes across an array of characters whose full time occupation is being "the bad guy" and they are very good at it. You come across drug money, drugs, gangs, violence, prostitution and other illegal activities. If a police officer is not careful these could seduce him or her to becoming a slave to the vices and find him or herself taking part in the very same activities that they are sworn to combat.

Ole Smooth was such a cool dude. He could have been an actor. Nothing rattled Ole Smooth. The word was that Ole Smooth had capped (shot) a burglar when he was a rookie. Ole Smooth did not talk much about the incident because he was just that kind of a guy. As we were cruising through the sixth district the dispatcher called us and I answered, "This is Beat 631." Ole Smooth got on the radio and said, "Give us one second squad." Ole Smooth looked at me with disdain, "Don't you ever answer the radio like that." He said, "When the dispatcher calls you, you say, squad, 631, what you got for me." I said, "What's the difference?" Ole Smooth said, "You sound like an uptight nerd and other officers could hear fear in your voice." We patrolled the streets for a few hours answering calls, and then we took a personal (15minute break) at his sister's house that resided in the sixth district. She looked at me and said, "You have got to be kidding me. Is anyone out there going to take you seriously? You are just a baby." Ole Smooth began to laugh and said, "You should have seen the shoes he was wearing."

I was twenty-four years old when I started working as a police officer and I guess she thought that I was just a child, and in retrospect I was. Nevertheless, I did not know how the people on the street viewed me; I just knew that I was going to be as safe as I could possibly be on the street. I was confident in my ability to do the job and besides I grew up in the "hood."

During my first few years as a police officer I received a lot of looks from "the bad guys" because I was so young. It was if one of them wanted to be the first to test me out.

As we were leaving Ole Smooth's sister's house she told me to make sure I listen to Ole Smooth because she didn't want me to get hurt and she said that I better be sure to back Ole smooth up at all times. I told her that I would be sure to do that. She looked at me and then shook her head in disbelief that I was a police officer and then closed the door. As we were leaving her house, Ole Smooth could sense that I was a little upset at the way his sister treated me. Ole Smooth said, "You are going to experience a little resistance from people because you are young and new on the job, but you have to talk to people in a manner that commands respect."

Big Bo Kicking Ass and Taking Names

A few hours later we responded to a call of a street disturbance. When we arrived on the scene people were screaming and shouting. There was broken glass and furniture lying on the grass. It was a very intimidating sight and there was a great deal of tension. My heart was pounding with nervous energy. I looked up and saw a very large lady with rollers in her hair throwing things from the apartment window. She threw a lamp out of the window and it just missed striking an officer in the head. One of the officers known as Big Bo charged up the stairs and we followed him.

Big Bo was a mighty warrior. He stood about six feet even and he had muscles all over his body. He was built like a Mack truck. Big Bo was a mellow guy, but he loved action. Big Bo liked to fish, cook and eat and he loved the dusties. Easy living was his first passion, and his second passion was being the "police." Big Bo would come to the locker room before his tour of duty, singing the Temptations, O'jays, Lou Rawls and a host of other old school Rhythm and Blues songs, and he could sing well! Big Bo's motto when making an arrest was, you can come easy or you can come hard. But I got the feeling that Big Bo enjoyed doing it the hard way.

Big Bo kicked in the door and charged toward the lady. Big Bo slapped her across the face and said, "Bitch you could have seriously injured a police officer." The woman spit in Bo's face and out of nowhere six men came out of a room and we were in for the fight of our lives. As one of the men tried to hit Big Bo, Monster met him with a right cross and he fell straight to the ground. As I was fighting one of the men, Ole Smooth grabbed him and twisted his arm back, he fell to the ground and we placed the handcuffs on him. Monster picked one of the men up by his throat and said, "Are you out of your damn mind? You bet not ever fuck with the police!" He slammed him to the floor and then put the handcuffs on him. I thought to myself, Monster is one mean bastard, and I am glad I'm on his side. We arrested everyone in that house.

As we were placing "the bad guys" in the wagon so that they could be transported to the sixth district station Big Bo told Monster, "Thanks for covering me." Monster said, "Nobody fucks with the police, and they bet not fuck with my home boy Big Bo!" Big Bo told Monster that when he got home tonight that he was going to cook some catfish and greens and sit down and watch some television in his underwear and after he finished eating, the television would be watching him. They laughed and Monster said, "Slam a cold one with me before you go to the crib." Big

Bo said, "Sounds good to me big fella." Big Bo was so mellow; I couldn't understand how he could be a friend of Monster.

When we got in the squad car Ole Smooth said, "This is what we call, kicking ass and taking names." Ole Smooth told me that the police never lose a fight. When I went home that night I called up my friends and told them the story and they asked me if I was going to continue working the job. I told them why not? I'm from Woodlawn!

First Felony Arrest

The first felony arrest that I made came shortly after that huge fight. I was writing a parking ticket on 79th and Cottage Grove when Ole Smooth and I received a call of a theft from auto at 850 East 83rd street. When we arrived on the scene a lady informed us that her vehicle had been broken into and some of her personal property was removed. She said the man was wearing all white, and he was. He had on a white shirt, white shorts, white socks and some white dress shoes. We toured the area and when we observed a man fitting this description. Ole Smooth said to me, "Watch this," he immediately notified the dispatcher and then we jumped out of the squad car, the offender looked at us and took off running.

Ole Smooth got on the radio again. He said, "631 emergency!" The dispatcher said, "Go with your emergency 631." Ole Smooth said, "I'm chasing the offender wanted in the theft. He's running northbound from 85th on Cottage Grove. He is a male black about 6 feet, wearing all white." The dispatcher relayed the information to the other officers in the district. We chased him for about a block and I finally caught him at 86th and Cottage Grove. I grabbed him around the neck and said, "It's over." Ole Smooth was right next to me. He looked at me and said, "This is how we do it." He slapped him across the head a few times and elbowed him in the throat. Ole Smooth said "Put the cuffs on him." I reached back into my gunbelt and removed my handcuffs and placed one of the cuffs around one of his wrists, but he kept moving. Ole Smooth grabbed his other hand and twisted it and I was able to handcuff him.

When we went back to the station to process the offender, many of the officers patted me on the back saying, "Good job rookie." Monster said, "So fucking what, you are still a punk ass rookie and don't you forget it!" Lovely Laura looked at me and smiled. I said to myself I like this job. Lovely Laura was fine as red wine and she had all the curves that men like.... Well, I like them!

After we finished processing the offender we left the station and got back into the squad car. I asked Ole Smooth to tell me about Lovely Laura. Ole Smooth looked at me and smiled. He said, "Smith, you can't handle a woman like that." I told him that I just thought that she was nice looking, but Ole Smooth said, "You are trying to fuck up already." Do you remember the three B's?" I replied, 3B's? Ole Smooth said, "Listen carefully, the broads, booze and bullets will get your ass in a heap of trouble and you definitely better be careful when you are trying to date a policewoman because they know all of the tricks."

I replied, "I just want to know if she is cool or not." Ole Smooth said, "Don't bullshit me son. I've been around a while, and I know when somebody has his nose open. I have been watching the way you look at her." Ole Smooth looked at me and shook his head. He pulled into Burger King and said, "What do you want for lunch?" I ordered a chicken sandwich and Ole Smooth ordered the same.

Getting Low Down and Dirty in 6

Ole Smooth and I had just finished eating lunch when we heard the call of a "Ten-One." This is a serious call because it says that an officer is in serious trouble. When there is a call of a "Ten-One" every officer in the district who is available will race to the aid of a fellow police officer. Ole Smooth and I ran to the vehicle and proceeded to the location. When we arrived on the scene we observed several officers running towards a huge gang fight. Monster was wrestling two men and his partner was being beat up by a gang of thugs. Ole Smooth and I ran straight towards his partner and pulled the guys off of him.

It was getting dark out and all I could hear was people screaming and the sound of sirens. Monster threw one of the men on the park bench and it knocked him out cold and he busted one of the gangbangers' eyes. I was a little startled and then Monster said, "Stop looking and kick some ass motherfucker!" I pulled out my nightstick and started swinging away.

We were striking the gangbangers with our clubs, and fighting and wrestling for our lives. There were so many officers on the scene, it seemed like the entire sixth district was there. We were fighting for at least fifteen minutes to restore order, but it seemed like forever. When we got back to the station, Monster said, "Now that's how we do it in the sixth district rookie!" Wondering if I could do this everyday, I left the station and headed to the squad car.

A Speedy Trial

When we got back into the squad car Ole Smooth said, "That's what we call a speedy trial." I said, "What do you mean?" Ole Smooth said, "Whenever some chump hits a police officer or whenever you catch an offender in the act of a violent crime and he resists arrest or if he runs from you make sure you rough him up a bit. It's called a speedy trial because you don't need to let the judge decide innocence or guilt because you already know he is guilty and so he deserves a speedy trial, that's the American way!"

Monster

Ole Smooth took off one day because he had to go to see his doctor and they assigned me to work with Monster. Monster told me not to speak to him unless it was an emergency. He told me to get the radio and the keys and meet him in the parking lot. When I picked up the radio and keys I went to the parking lot and Monster was standing by the squad car. He said, "I will drive and answer the radio, you just be quiet and keep your eyes open for trouble." I said, "Cool." Typically the person who drives the squad car has that as the primary responsibility and the passenger is responsible for answering the radio and writing the police reports. We checked the vehicle to make sure it was safe and ready for our tour of duty. I got in the car and put on my seat belt. Monster said, "What the fuck are you doing?" I said I'm just putting on my seat belt. He said, "So when we see one of these little bastards trying to run from the police, you mean to tell me that I have to wait for your rookie ass to take off that seatbelt?" Before I could say anything he said, "Take that shit off and roll down the windows." Monster just frowned at me and said, "I have drawls older than you."

Monster and I made several traffic stops that night. But one stop is etched in my mind. We pulled over a red Chevy, which had expired plates, and inside the car were two men wearing red bandanas. The driver said, "Monster I know my plates are expired, but I am going to get them renewed tomorrow." Monster searched the guy, and found some marijuana in his front pocket. Monster looked at the guy and told him that he better have his plates up to date tomorrow because if he didn't he was going to have hell to pay. Monster then put the weed in his pocket and drove away. I said, "Monster why didn't we arrest him and inventory the marijuana." Monster said, "I told you not to say a damn thing to me. I don't talk to rookies." I kept my mouth closed and just stared out the passenger side window.

I was thinking to myself, what in the world is wrong with this dude? I thought we were on the same side. Why is he such an asshole to me? I have never done anything to him. As I was looking out of the window, I could just feel him staring at me. I turned around and he was looking at me with a serious scowl on his face. I just turned my head and looked straight ahead. He said, "That's more like it." and drove off.

Respect

We received a call of a domestic disturbance and when we arrived on the scene a teenage boy let us in the apartment. There was a couple arguing and they didn't stop when they saw us. I said, "Miss, we got a call here, what's the problem?" The lady was about 5feet 6. She had on a green sweat suit. She said, "You see the problem, this short fucker spent all of his money at the track and we can't pay the damn rent." Her husband who stood about 5feet even said, "I told her that I would have the money next week." They continued to argue with each other and Monster just looked at me. I was thinking to myself, what do I do now? Monster walked over to a brown wooden table and grabbed a vase and threw it on the floor and it shattered. The lady said to him, "What the hell are you doing?" Monster said, "What the hell are you doing?" I have real police work to do and you call me because you are tired of this little bity sawed off motherfucker that you are married to." The man did not say a word. He went to the kitchen and the lady told us to get the hell out of her house. When we got back into the squad car Monster said, "You see how they just ignored your punk ass, but I get results." I was about to ask Monster how to handle a situation like that but I thought about it and just remained quiet.

Monster looked at me and said, "You don't look like the police. You are a little clean-shaven kid. You need to get tough and you need to be physical out here. You need to lift some weights because you are going to have to knock a motherfucker out on these streets. I know Ole Smooth is training you right, but I will show you what it takes to get respect out here." I was on pins and needles the entire afternoon I worked with Monster.

Funny Shit

We responded to a call of a street disturbance on the other end of the district. Monster turned on the emergency lights and began to drive like a mad man. He was weaving in and out of traffic and I was holding on for dear life. I saw another car coming straight toward us and I shouted, "Monster look out!" He said, "I see that fucking car, that motherfucker better watch me." We escaped a collision because the other car was able to stop. Monster didn't even attempt to put his foot on the brakes. He scared the living hell out of me!

When we arrived on the scene we saw two men arguing. Monster said, "What's the problem?" One of the men told Monster that the man he was arguing with was cheating on him. Monster said, "What the fuck are you talking about?" The man said that they were lovers and he caught his boyfriend cheating on him. Monster looked at them and said, "You have to be pulling my fucking leg. I don't give a damn about who's cheating on who, but you little bitches better take this shit inside because I have real police work to do." I tapped Monster on the shoulder and said, "Take it easy bro." Monster looked at me as if to say shut the hell up. He turned toward the men and said, "Now get off the fucking street before I shove my nightstick up your ass, but then again yall might like that." The men looked at Monster and just walked away.

When we got back into the squad car Monster started laughing. He said, "You see some funny shit on this job." Trying to make conversation and be friendly, I asked Monster what was the funniest thing he had ever seen and he stopped laughing and looked at me and said, "Shut the fuck up. I was talking to myself and if you ever tell me to cool out when I'm doing my job, I will beat your kid cop ass!" I replied, "Monster I just didn't think you should talk to people like that. It's very disrespectful." Monster said, "I don't give a damn about what you are talking about! Save the shit for somebody with a heart!" All of a sudden we received a call of an officer needs assistance.

When we arrived on the scene Lovely Laura and her partner Sweet Rose were breaking up a fight. Monster walked up and asked them who needs to go to jail. Lovely Laura said, "I tried to get this man to leave but he insisted on arguing with us." Monster looked at the men and they didn't say a word. Monster said, "I want you to apologize to these fine officers." The men apologized and Monster said, "When the police tell you to do something, you better do it." The men replied, "Yes sir." Monster told them to get off the street and they left in a hurry. Monster was well known in the district for being one mean ass policeman.

About a week later I received a complaint register number regarding the domestic disturbance call I handled with Monster. A complaint register number is a complaint that a citizen has filed against an officer for improper conduct such as verbal or physical abuse. I approached Monster and asked him what I should write in reply to the accusations. Monster said, "I told you that I do not talk to rookies go wipe your ass with that complaint." I talked to Ole Smooth and he told me what to write. He told me that I would be fine. I said, "Why is Monster such an asshole?" Ole Smooth said, 'He is just from the old school and he hates rookies." Ole Smooth told me that once I finished my first year on the job and was no longer on probation that I will see a different side of him.

Important Addresses

One day we responded to a call of a domestic disturbance. We arrived on the scene and entered the apartment. The couple was arguing with each other, using every bad word they could come up with. We tried to talk to them but they kept on arguing. Ole smooth went into the kitchen and opened up the refrigerator took out an egg and began frying it. The couple immediately stopped arguing and looked at Ole Smooth. He asked them how long they have been married. They said, "Twenty-five years." Ole Smooth said, "What's the problem?" They looked at each other and told us that we could leave because they would work it out. Ole Smooth had a way of making things look easy.

When we got back in the squad car I asked Ole Smooth had he ever did anything like that before during his career? Ole Smooth said, "You have to be creative our here. I could tell by their tone of voice that they weren't really angry with each other and so I dealt with it like I did." I told Ole Smooth that I thought he did a good job. Ole Smooth said, "Who is training who here?" Ole Smooth said, "This is what I do."

At that very moment we heard a call of a burglary in progress at Big Bo's home. Ole Smooth said, "Hold on, that's Bo's crib, it's time to rock and roll." Ole Smooth turned on the lights and sirens and we hurried to the location. When we arrived we heard the dispatcher give a slowdown. A slowdown alerts officers to take their time in coming to assist because the situation has been diffused. The dispatcher said, "Units in the sixth district we have officers on the scene so take it easy, don't get yourselves hurt going over there, Beat 622 is calling a slowdown and has everything under control." Ole Smooth and I entered the house and we saw Big Bo slapping the living hell out of the offender. Monster put on his black leather gloves and said, "Big Bo let your boy get some." Monster looked at the guy and said, "You then fucked up now!" Monster hit him right on top of the head and he fell to the floor. He said, "I'm sorry for breaking in your house." Big Bo said, "You like going through windows huh?" He told Monster and a few of the other officers to go out in the backyard because this dude likes going through windows. They proceeded to the back yard and Big Bo picked the guy up and threw him out of the window. They took him back inside the house and finished his speedy trial.

Ole Smooth said, "You have to get to know some important addresses in the district because we have police officers living here in the sixth district, and you definitely have to have our district commanders address memorized because he also lives in the district. If you ever here a call at his address you better haul ass and get there!" I told Ole Smooth that I definitely appreciate his training and advice.

Ole Smooth said, "I bet you that fool a think twice about breaking into someone's house again. Did you see the look on his face when he saw all of us in the house?" I told Ole Smooth that he looked like a deer in headlights. We laughed as we headed into the station to see the watch commander.

Shots Fired

Captain Burnside told Ole Smooth that he wanted us to ride along with the tact team to serve a warrant. There must always be a unit in uniform when the plain-clothes tactical unit serves a warrant. Captain Burnside said, "Smith this will be a good learning experience for you." Ole Smooth and I proceeded to the location. When we arrived there were about eight to ten tactical officers. When the tact team saw Ole Smooth and I in uniform they said, "Let's do this." We all drew are guns and four members of the tact team busted the door open with a sledgehammer. When we got there people were scattering to get rid of their drugs and weapons. The tact team arrested everyone in the house. They thanked Ole Smooth and then called the police wagon to transport "the bad guys" to the police station for processing.

The next day Ole Smooth tells me that he is going to let me drive. He said, "It's time for you to get familiar with driving the squad car." I was excited. I said, "Cool let me see what I can do." After we received our keys and radios we went to the parking lot and I did the usual check of the squad car. I checked the back seat to make sure nothing was left from the previous tour and more importantly no weapons or drugs. I checked the tires to make sure they were inflated properly and I made sure the emergency equipment was working. Ole Smooth got into the passenger seat and we were ready to roll.

I was driving slowly at 79th and Halsted when I heard, "632 emergency!" The dispatcher responded, "Go ahead with your emergency 632." Squad I hear shots fired at 87th and Ashland." I turned on the emergency lights and started driving to the location. Ole Smooth looked at me and said, "You are going to have to drive faster than that." I placed my foot on the accelerator and I looked at the speedometer and it read 90mph. Ole Smooth shouted, "Keep you damn eyes on the road!" I lifted my head and saw that I was about to run into the intersection. Ole Smooth said, "You have to slow down when you approach an intersection, especially when the light is red."

Ole Smooth said, "Look to your right and then look to your left. Now blow the horn, and ease out so they can see you." I did just as Ole Smooth had instructed. When the other vehicles had stopped Ole Smooth said, "Now let's roll!" I put my foot down on the accelerator and we were off. When we arrived on the scene we saw a crowd gathering. Beat 632 said, "Squad we have a bona fide shooting at 87th and Ashland, could you send an ambulance?" We helped the other officers there to move back the people so that we could secure the crime scene. As we forced our way through we saw a young African-American man lying on the ground holding his leg. I saw blood oozing from his pants leg. We began to ask the people on the scene if they had seen anything but nobody volunteered any information. The young man who had been shot refused to tell us anything when we questioned him. Beat 632 followed him to the hospital to make out the report and to see if they could ascertain any pertinent information. Ole Smooth and I continued to ask questions but no one told us anything.

Ole Smooth told me that it was common for some of the guys who are gang affiliated to remain quiet when they have been shot by a rival gang. He informed me that the guy who was shot would retaliate by shooting him or a member of his gang. Ole Smooth said, "Our work here is done. We will let beat 632 and the detectives handle it from here." I am thinking to myself that this doesn't make any sense. Angry and wondering why there is so much violence in the African-American community I headed back to the squad car.

Chapter 2

Englewood Ranger

Danger is never a stranger to an Englewood Ranger

Upon finishing my field training Captain Burnside called Ole Smooth and me into his office. He said, "Smith your field training is over with and you are assigned to the seventh district (Englewood)." I looked at Ole Smooth and he looked at me and he began to laugh. I had heard that Englewood was one of the toughest districts in the city, but I still didn't know what lay ahead. Captain Burnside laughed also, and said, "Smith you will be fine, and you are a young strong officer. Just remember what Ole Smooth taught you and your experience here." Capitan Burnside was a good man. I told him that I really enjoyed the training I received in the sixth district, and that Ole Smooth is like a big brother to me. Ole Smooth and Captain Burnside were laughing because they knew that Englewood is one of the roughest districts in the City of Chicago.

There is saying, which goes, "Danger is never a stranger to an Englewood ranger." How true this is. I would come to find out that Englewood is an interesting community. There is a great deal of violence that occurs in the district and a lot of calls regarding disturbances with mentally ill persons. When an officer receives a call of a disturbance with a mental you can bet your life that you are in for either an exercise in verbal virtuosity or the fight of your life.

I can remember my first day in Englewood. As I walked to the police station a friend from the police academy who did his field training in Englewood approached me. He told me to remove the administrative services from my nametag and replace it with the one that reads 007th district. All probationary police officers (rookies with less than one year on the job) were required to wear this tag. But my friend in his wisdom told me that "the bad guys" know you are new when they see that tag. Therefore, my first order of business was to find a nametag, which read 007th district.

I worked the first watch (midnight to eight in the morning) my first month in Englewood and I thought I was living in the Wild Wild West. I didn't have a problem staying up because "the bad guys" were up all night. We receive calls for disturbances, fights, shots fired all night long. I thought to myself, I am from the hood but this is unreal. I can't believe that people actually live like this.

The streets of Chicago are rough and Englewood is no joke! I found the people I worked with to be very interesting. Each officer has his or her way of going about his or her work. Some officers are extremely aggressive making several traffic stops during a tour of duty and others are more relaxed, answering their calls and making sure they protect themselves and constantly backing up other officers. I contend that I fell into the latter category. The streets are dangerous and I saw no reason to put myself in harm's way, especially when we were constantly receiving calls of shots fired, aggravated battery, domestic battery, robbery in progress. I didn't have time to look for anything extra because danger was always a radio call away. When I first started out on the police department I vowed to be respectful and kind to everyone, but after several unique experiences I adopted the motto, "Kick ass and take names!" It was the only way that I could survive and keep my sanity on the streets.

One of the most interesting things that I found out from being a police officer is how fast things can happen. One of the lieutenants used to say, "SHIT" can get not so funny real fast." One minute the radio is quiet and you're just riding around thinking about things that you need to do, and then the next minute somebody is shot.

Frantic Frank

I was working one night with Frantic Frank. Frantic Frank was extremely aggressive. We all have 24 hours in a day, but Frantic Frank's 24 hours moved at a quicker pace. If there were three hands on the wristwatch of life, Frantic Frank would be the third hand, constantly moving. Just when you think that you have figured him out, Frantic Frank was already on to the next number of arrests, and he made a lot of them.

I imagine that he, unlike many of us, uses up every minute of the day and every inch of his 5ft 5-inch frame thinking, dreaming, and breathing police. When I first met him I thought he was insane. No surprise to anyone Frantic Frank responded to every call that he could. I'm not talking about just the calls that he received. I'm talking about every call that any other officer received. Frantic Frank was quick to appear on any given scene, there were times when you could catch him long enough to notice the leather fingers of a pair of black gloves dangling from his back pocket, itching and snapping in anticipation of the next arrest.

Frantic Frank made a least fifty traffic stops a night. The first night that I worked with him he said, "What's up rookie? How do you like the job?" I said, "It's very interesting. It seems like the craziness never ends." Frantic Frank looked at me and let out one of the loudest laughs I have ever heard. He said, "You got that right Smith. It never ends, and I hope it doesn't because that means that I would have to get a real job!" We pulled out of the parking lot and made a left on Racine and continued driving northbound until we reached 55th street. All of a sudden, Frantic Frank pulled over a black Pontiac without any state license plates and as we approached the car with our guns drawn, Frantic Frank said to the driver, "Turn off the vehicle and show me your hands." As we got closer the driver immediately pulled off. I notified the dispatcher that two subjects were fleeing in a black Pontiac without license plates eastbound across 55th street from Racine. We jumped back into the squad car and chased "The bad guys" east on 55th. Other squad cars joined in on the chase. We eventually caught the offenders at 71st and Yale. Frantic Frank took out his flashlight and struck one of "the bad guys" in the head and he began to bleed profusely, but it seemed as if he did not even feel it. We handcuffed the subjects and searched the car but we didn't find anything in the vehicle or on their person, but we could smell marijuana and alcohol on their breath and so we took them into custody.

Dead On Arrival

When we finished processing these guys we left the station and drove around for about 30 minutes and all of a sudden we hear shots fired around 59th and Aberdeen. I notified the dispatcher, I said, "Squad this is beat 715, we are hearing shots fired in the area of 59th and Aberdeen." We drove up and down the block on Aberdeen and then turned into the alley and that's when we saw a man lying in the street. We approached him with our guns drawn. When we got up close we could see that he had been shot in the head. We notified the ambulance and they came and took him to the hospital. The man was dead on arrival.

Frantic Frank and I looked around to see if we could locate some clues as to who had shot the man, but we could not find anything or anyone who would say that they saw what had occurred. Frantic Frank told me that he believed that the man was killed as a part of the retaliation for a shooting that had occurred the previous day. Frantic Frank told me that I needed to be very careful on the streets. He said, "There have been a lot of gang related shootings in the past month and you have to be careful that you don't windup in a cross-fire." Frantic Frank is a good police officer. He is fair with "the bad guys"…well about as fair as one can be. More importantly, he always looks out for his fellow officers.

Mad Max

One afternoon I was working with one of the craziest guys in the district known as Mad Max. Mad Max had led the district in arrest the previous year. Mad Max was in his mid-thirties and he had ten years on the police department. He stood about six feet even, he had brown hair and he was clean-shaven and he always wore black combat boots. He was a very unassuming guy, but he was hell on the street. His reputation preceded him. Mad Max knew most of "the bad guys" in the district and they knew him! When Max went to a call order was restored very rapidly. Mad Max loved being a police officer and besides his extreme tactics, I must say he that he was pretty good one.

We received a call of a man selling drugs on 59th and Ashland. When we arrived on the scene we approached several men on the street. Mad Max asked them what was going on out here and they just said that they were just cooling out. Mad Max called a guy over fitting the description and began to search him. When he did not find anything in his pockets Mad Max grabbed him by the throat and began to choke him. I said, "Max take it easy," but as soon as I spoke those words a bag of crack cocaine came out of "the bad guy's" mouth as he was being choked. Mad Max told me to search the area and we recovered several bags of crack cocaine from underneath a brick that concealed a deep hole in the grass where the drugs were buried.

When we got into the car I told Mad Max that I was sorry for interfering with him. I said, "It looked like the man couldn't breathe and I didn't want you to kill him." Mad Max just stared at me. After a few minutes Mad Max said, "I know that you were in school studying to be a priest, but you better leave that bullshit to Fr. Flanagan. Don't you ever tell me to stop doing my job! This shit is real out here! Your college degree don't mean a damn thing in the Wood, you better get your street degree if you plan on being the police." I said, "Mad Max, you scared me and I froze up. I really thought that you were choking the man." Mad Max said, "I was choking his ass! And what happened? He coughed up the damn dope." Mad Max said, "Smith I know a little about your background. I know you didn't grow up in the lily-white suburbs, but you have still been sheltered. You will find out real fast that the streets of Englewood are a world of its own. And in this world there are no chumps allowed!"

Mad Max told me that he respects me, but "the bad guys" on the street don't. He said that I need to develop a no-nonsense attitude on the street. Mad Max said, "You have to let these punks know that you will beat the living shit out of them if you have to." I asked Mad Max if it was easier just to talk to them and get them to see our point of view. Mad Max said that "the bad guys" don't respect someone being nice to them. Mad Max said, "They know that I will put my foot in their ass, that's why I get respect. Smith, you better get tough. You need to develop a reputation for kicking ass out here because if you don't you will get punked out." Mad Max said, "I can tell you are a little nervous on some of these calls but you have to lose that fear. When I walk on the scene I am thinking that I will kick anybody's ass that even looks at me the wrong way and you have to develop this attitude and it will become a part of who you are."

I told Mad Max that I understand where he is coming from and that I will make sure I am focused at all times. I said, "When you were choking the guy I saw tears come from his eyes and he began to shake. It just really made me nervous. I didn't want him to die." Mad Max said, "It's good that you saw this because now you know how sneaky and tricky these punks can be. I knew that he had the dope in his mouth because I have been doing this shit a long time. They can't fool me. Smith you need to develop a killer instinct on the streets. You have to match violence with more violence. If a motherfucker hits you once you hit him three times!" I told Max that I understand his point.

The Mental

Mad Max and I responded to call of a disturbance with a mental which another beat car was assigned to. When we arrived on the scene I saw the offender pick up a fellow officer and throw him down from the front stairs. We charged the offender with our nightsticks drawn, Mad Max struck him in the head several times but he was still fighting as blood was dripping from his head. I hit him in the head with the butt of my nightstick over and over again. It took eight officers to restrain and arrest this offender but we finally got the cuffs on him.

When we got back to the squad car Mad Max said, "Now that's what the fuck I'm talking about! I don't care how crazy that motherfucker is, I bet that ass whipping will make him think straight now. You see what I mean Smith? You did a good job of pounding that sack of shit. That's what I mean by no-nonsense!" I was thinking to myself that I was just fighting to survive and that I really didn't enjoy what I did. I didn't join the police department to hurt anyone but it seems like this was par for the course.

When I finished my tour of duty that day I was extremely tired. We had responded to over thirty calls that night. Mad Max taught me a valuable lesson; you can't be nice on the streets unless you want to get hurt. I went home thinking about being a police officer. I was asking myself if I had the mind set to deal with other human beings in this manner. I don't enjoy hurting anyone, but I don't want anyone to hurt me.

It's Show Time

About a month later I got off duty and checked the assignment sheet for the next day and saw that I would be working with Mad Max. I went down to the locker room to change into my civilian clothes. I left the station and crossed the street to the parking lot to get into my vehicle. Mad Max was standing next to my car. He said, "Smith you're working with me tomorrow so you better get some rest." He reached into his pocket and pulled out a pair of bronzed brass knuckles. He said, "These are for you, and you better not lose them." As I drove home all I could think about was working with Mad Max. I only got two hours of sleep that night because all I could think about was Mad Max and his antics.

I tossed and turned all night because I knew that I was in for a long day. I could hear Mad Max's voice in my sleep, "You better get tough Smith. It's time to kick some ass!" I was still new on the job and so I was still adjusting to being a police officer, and when you work with a guy like Mad Max you have to expect the unexpected.

When I arrived at roll-call the next day Mad Max was talking to some other officers about the arrest he made the previous night. He looked at me and said, "You ready Smith?" And I said, "Damn right," but all along I am thinking that this is one crazy Son of a bitch! When we left roll-call and got into the vehicle, Mad Max said, "Do you have all of your equipment?" I said, "yes." Mad Max looked me up and down and then said, "Show me your fist." I made a fist and looked at him. Max said, "That's not a fist." He reached into his pocket and slipped on his brass knuckles and said, "Now this is a fist! Now show me yours!" I told Max that I left mine at home. Mad Max said, "Smith you better leave that choirboy shit at home." He got on the radio and said, "Squad hold us down for an equipment adjustment." Mad Max drove me to my apartment so that I could get my brass knuckles.

Mad Max said, "Smith I told you about being tough out here." I told Mad Max that I agree with him and that I have been kicking ass and taking names, but Mad Max said, "The brass knuckles that I gave you should be a part of your uniform because they have a way of restoring peace." I told Mad Max that I didn't think about bringing them because I didn't know that we could use them. Mad Max said, "Fuck that shit Smith! You better use them if you want to survive. Those sons of bitches in the training academy aren't out here fighting. When you use that academy shit that's when you will get hurt. Do you ever think that I tell "the bad guy" please step back sir? Hell no, I pull out my fucking stick and start peeling some fucking heads and they know to stay back! You have to put your hands on a motherfucker to let him know that you mean business." All along I am wonder if I have the mindset for this job. I want to help people and not hurt them.

When we got back into the district Mad Max grabbed his radio and said, "Squad this is 715, what you got for us?" The dispatcher said, Beat 715 we are getting a call of a street disturbance on 57th and Marshfield. Mad Max said, "We're on it squad." When we arrived on the scene the fight stopped and the people involved began to scatter. A lady approached us with a bandage on her head and a black eye and informed us that one of the guys involved in the fight beat her up yesterday. She pulled out the police report and showed it to us. She said, "There he is running in the blue shirt." Mad Max drove down the street, and when we got close to him Mad Max put the car in park and we jumped out of the vehicle and chased the guy down. Mad Max tackled him and we handcuffed him and he looked at Mad Max and said, "Mad Max, I didn't do anything." Mad Max said, "Well why are you running?" Mad Max searched him and inside of his underwear he had a brown paper bag full of marijuana. He said, "Mad Max, can you give me a break? Its just weed." Mad Max said, "I would but I don't like guys who beat up on women."

Mad Max asked the man if he would like it if somebody beat up his mother and before he could answer Mad Max elbowed him in the jaw. Mad Max looked at me and said, "What would you do if somebody like this asshole abused your mother or your sister?" Looking at Mad Max, I think to myself I am starting to understand this guy. I told Mad Max that I definitely understand where he is coming from.

Dunkin' Donuts

As soon as we left the station from doing the paper work from our arrest, Mad Max asked me if I was ready to take lunch. I was more than ready, but I was surprised. I didn't think a guy like Mad Max had time to take lunch because he was so busy looking for his next arrest. Mad Max asked me where I wanted to go for lunch. I told him that it didn't matter because I wasn't hungry but we could take lunch so I can cool out for a minute. Mad Max said he wasn't hungry either. He said, "Let's go to Dunkin' Donuts for some coffee." I told Mad Max that Dunkin' Donuts is good for me.

When we arrived at Dunkin' Donuts the manger pointed to a man walking down the street. He informed us that the man just shattered the glass door. We walked outside and the man looked back at us and then took off running northbound from 61st street on Western Avenue. Mad Max and I started chasing the man. When we caught up to him Mad Max grabbed the man by the neck and said, "What the hell did you break that glass for?" The man didn't say one word. Mad Max said, "Take care of him." I took out my handcuffs and began to place them on "the bad guys" wrist. Mad Max said, "What the hell are you doing?" I replied, "I'm placing the cuffs on him." Mad Max said, "Watch this." He slapped the man about the head several times and said, "If you ever do something like this again I am going to step on your fucking head." We took the man back to Dunkin' Donuts and we went inside and the manager told us that this man was angry with him because he didn't give him a free cup of coffee. The manager told us that the man comes in everyday begging his customers for money. The manager said that he wanted the man arrested for shattering his glass door. We weren't in our district so Mad Max notified the dispatcher to send an eighth district beat car to arrest the man and fill out the paperwork.

The manager gave us a free cup of coffee and we headed back to the seventh district. Mad Max looked at me and said, "Smith when I say take care of someone that means kick some ass!" I said, "We had the man in custody and I didn't think it was necessary for me to put my hands on him." Mad Max shook his head and said, "You are going to learn how to do this job sooner or later." There was a brief silence before Mad Max shouted, "I love this job. Other than being a professional athlete where else can you work and have this much fun? We do a lot of good things out here and the average person doesn't know the things that we have to put up with." When we got back to the district, Mad Max told the dispatcher that we were ready to rock and roll. The dispatcher said, "That's great Beat 715. Can you take a ride on the other end of the district for a disturbance on 57th and Shields?" I said, "Ten-four squad." ("Ten-four" acknowledges a message received) And Mad Max hurried to the location. When we arrived on the scene we saw a man holding a rag to his head. We approached him and we noticed that blood was oozing from his head. He told us that he was playing basketball and somebody elbowed him in the head. He told us that he was cool, but we needed to go inside of the recreation center because there was a fight inside.

Let Me Put on My Shirt

We ran inside and there were two men fighting. I yelled, "Break it up," but Mad Max said, "Let them duke it out, that way it will be easier for us to deal with it." The men fought for about five more minutes before Mad Max and I pulled them apart. Mad Max said, "Who needs to go to jail?" The men who were fighting said that it was settled and that nobody needs to go to jail. Mad Max told them to leave the gym and the left in a hurry.

When we left the disturbance on Shields, we were driving Westbound on Garfield when a lady told us that her boyfriend had beaten her up. She told us that he was still in the apartment. I told Mad Max that we should call the dispatcher since this address is in the ninth district. Mad Max said, "What does your star say?" Before I could answer he said, "Chicago Police." We got out of the vehicle and followed the lady to her apartment. Mad Max said, "I want you to do the talking, but you know I got your back." I asked the lady if she had any weapons in the house and she told me no.

We entered the apartment and her boyfriend was sitting on the couch wearing a red bandana, no shirt and some blue jeans. I said, "Sir your girlfriend wants you to leave the apartment. She said, "Hell naw, I want his ass arrested for hitting me." I looked at Mad Max but he was keeping a close eye on the boyfriend. I said, "Sir I need you to stand up." He said, "I didn't touch this tramp, she is just mad because she saw me with my baby's momma last night." The lady's sister said, "He smacked her in the face and pushed her to the ground." I said, "You are going to have to go with us." The man said, "Ok, let me put on my shirt and I will come but I didn't touch this bitch." The man stood up and told us that he was going to the room to get a shirt. We followed him into the room, but when he went into his room he picked up a lamp and threw it at us and tried to run out the back door. Mad Max and I took off running after him. We caught him right at the rear door. Mad Max grabbed him by the throat and pushed his head against the door. Mad Max grabbed his right arm and placed his handcuffs around his right wrist. I grabbed his left arm and we handcuffed him and took him to the squad car.

The "Real Police"

It was getting close to quitting time when we heard a female officer screaming for help. "713 emergency: I am chasing a male black wanted for robbery. He's running westbound across 62nd from Halsted." Mad Max drove to the scene and we saw officers Sweet Ann and Sultry Suzy running after the offender. Mad Max said, "Watch this." While the offender was running Mad Max pulled up behind him and bumped him with the vehicle. The man was lifted up on top of the hood of the squad car. Mad Max and I got out of the car and Mad Max said, "Do your thing Smith." I twisted the man's arm back and slapped him in the face. He said, "What the fuck did yall hit me for?" I said, "Don't ever run from the police." Mad Max and I got the cuffs on him and we took him back to the station. When we got into the station, Mad Max told a few of the other officers that I was becoming the "real police." They looked at me and nodded their heads in affirmation. I said to myself I like this feeling. I made a vow to become a no-nonsense police officer because that's how you get things done in the Wood. Mad Max and I received an honorable mention for capturing a man who robbed a liquor store while armed with a handgun.

Mad Max looked at me and said, Smith I am beginning to like you. I said, "Thanks Mad Max." Mad Max replied, "What are you still doing with that bullshit revolver? It's nice to have but you better get some more firepower because these assholes on the street have some serious heat. And look at your coat." I said, "What's wrong with it?" Mad Max said, "It's a pussy's jacket. You need to get a leather jacket because it's intimidating." I went to Kales uniform store the next day and bought a leather jacket. I went to Shore Galleries in Skokie and looked for a semi-automatic handgun. One of the salesmen said that I should try shooting a few of the guns on the practice range. I said fine. I fired the Glock, Ruger, Smith & Wesson and the Beretta. I purchased the Beretta nine-millimeter handgun, because I liked it the best and I wanted to be ready for the bad guys.

When I fell in for roll-call, Mad Max looked at me and told me to see him after roll-call. I approached him and said, "What's the deal Mad Max?" He said, "I'm glad you got your new gun and leather jacket; you are starting to look like the police." We got our equipment and headed to the squad car. Mad Max drove to a vacant lot and parked the car. He said, "Take off your jacket." I removed my radio from the clip and took off my jacket and gave it to Mad Max. Mad Max looked at it and said, "This is nice, but it needs some work." I told Mad Max that I didn't understand what he was talking about. Mad Max said, "Take everything out of your pockets." I removed my Fraternal Order of Police handbook and my brass knuckles and gave my jacket to Mad Max. Mad Max got out of the squad car and placed my jacket on the ground and he ran over it about ten times with the squad car. He gave it back to me and it was dirty and the leather was scratched. Mad Max said, "Now you are ready. You look like you will beat the living shit out of one of these criminals."

I wasn't the least bit upset. I told Mad Max that he was my hero on the police department because nobody showed me the ropes like him. My field-training officer Ole Smooth taught me a great deal, but Mad Max showed me how to put fear in a criminal's heart!

We were patrolling around 57th and Marshfield when I asked Mad Max if he was ever scared out here on the streets. Mad Max was quiet for about two minutes, and then he looked at me and said, "Smith I'm not going to lie to you. When I first came on the job I was nervous because I saw some scary looking motherfuckers out here that didn't mind fighting the police, as a matter a fact, they loved it. But I said to myself that I am here to uphold the law and so I have to put fear behind me. I knew that I had to be very aggressive to survive the streets of Englewood." Mad Max told me that he was injured on duty when he responded to a street disturbance and as he was trying to break up the fight he suffered a broken arm. Mad Max told me that you must always be ready to split one of these bastards head, because if you don't they will split yours.

No More Probation

I finished my year on the job and I was no longer a probationary police officer. I was happy. I said to myself that I am the real police now and the ink is finally dry on my application. I went to work the following day and the watch commander Captain hard guy said "Congratulations Smith, you completed your first year on the job, but remember this, you still have a lot to learn and you won't fully comprehend policing until you have spent at least five years on the street."

I told Captain hard guy that I really enjoy working with Mad Max because he is showing me the ropes. Captain hard guy said, "I'm glad you are enthusiastic about learning. Mad Max is a good officer. He will show you the things you need to do to be safe and successful out here."

Lovely Laura

A few weeks later lovely Laura calls me and says since you are a big boy now I am going to let you hang out with me. I was so excited! Every time I looked at Lovely Laura my heart would beat fast. She told me to come and pick her up and she was going to take me out to dinner. I went to Lovely Laura's house and when she answered the door she was dressed in a beautiful red dress. She said, "I am glad that you came to see me." All I could do was smile.

Lovely Laura asked me if I wanted anything to drink. I asked her if she had any beer. She gave me a cold Heineken and asked me if I wanted a glass. I told her that I like drinking my beer out of the bottle. Lovely Laura asked me if I was dating anyone. I told her that I have a girlfriend from college, but we are having some rough times because of my job. I asked Lovely Laura if she was dating anybody, when all of a sudden I heard a knock on the door. Lovely Laura didn't answer; she just motioned for me to be quiet. Then a loud voice exclaimed, "Laura, answer the damn door!" I whispered, "I know that voice. Laura looked at me and I said, "that's Monster". My heart was beating fast as hell. I was scared to leave. I waited until 3:00AM in the morning before I left Lovely Laura's house because I thought by that time the coast would be clear.

As I left Lovely Laura's house someone comes out from behind the bushes in front of her house and grabs me from behind and begins choking the life out of me. He said, "You better keep your ass away from this house." It was Monster. I couldn't say anything because I couldn't breathe. All of a sudden I hear Lovely Laura say, "Monster put him down, that's Smith." Monster let me go and told me to stay away from his woman. I told Monster that I didn't know that they were dating and I got into my car and went home.

Lovely Laura called me the next day to apologize. I said, "Why didn't you tell me you were dating Monster." Lovely Laura said that they dated a few years ago and that Monster is married, and that Monster is good to her financially. She said that if she ever needs anything that Monster would get it for her. She asked if we were still cool and I said, "Of course, but I am terrified of Monster." Lovely Laura told me not to worry about Monster because she would handle him.

The very next day Lovely Laura tells me to meet her at the Den for some drinks. When I walked in she was sitting at a table with Monster. I started to turn around and leave, but she called my name and motioned for me to come and join them. I went to the table and sat down. Monster asked me what I wanted to drink. I replied, "Jack on the rocks." Monster went to the bar. I asked Lovely Laura why she asked me to meet her while she was with this crazy bastard. She said that Monster wanted to tell me something. Monster returned with three shots of Jack Daniels.

Lovely Laura excused herself and went to the ladies room. Monster said, "Look, I'm sorry for choking you the other day, I didn't know that was you but Lovely Laura is mine and you just need to stay away from her." Monster handed me my drink and he took his and he said, "Let's toast to you finding you a woman and leaving mine alone." We drank the whiskey straight down. Monster reached into his pocket and pulled out a one hundred dollar bill. He gave it to me and said, "Go get you some pussy, because Lovely Laura is off limits." I took the one hundred dollars and left the Den.

Lovely Laura called me the next day and said that I was her favorite little man and that she appreciated me for understanding her situation. I told Lovely Laura that I would love to hang out with her, but Monster is a man that I don't want to mess with. She said that I would always be her little chocolate buttercup. I told her that she was just so outstanding to me but I don't want to be involved in a soap opera. Lovely Laura just laughed and said, "I understand where you are coming from, but we will see each other soon." I said, "We will see." Lovely Laura said, "See you later little man." I then hung the phone up and hit the streets.

Little Dope Boy

I was so tired one morning after getting off of midnights but I had to go to traffic court for the tickets that I had written. While I was in court waiting for my cases to be called I started to doze off. The judge told the sheriff to wake me up. The judge said, "You need to stay awake in my court room." I apologized to the judge and told him that I had just finished my tour of duty. The judge said, "You are not the only officer here who just got off work, what district are you in?" I replied, "Englewood your honor." The judge said, "Pull officer Smith's cases next." I was so happy because I was able to go home and get some much-needed rest.

I made my first solo narcotics arrest when I saw a boy about 15 years old hand a young lady a small bag and then receive some money from her. I got out of the squad car and as soon as he saw me he dropped a plastic bag to the ground. I approached him and put the cuffs on him and then I recovered a bag, which contained about 10 packets of crack cocaine. I searched him but I didn't find anything on him. He said, "That's not mine." I said I saw you drop it to the ground. He said, "You can't prove a got damn thing." I took him in the station and notified the youth officer. When the youth officer cam into the station, he looked at the guy and said, "What's up Bushwick?" He told me that Bushwick is always in trouble.

I went to court the next day and Bushwick had an attorney that was known for representing the dope dealers. This attorney sliced my testimony apart and the judge let Bushwick go. When I went to work later that afternoon I was patrolling my beat and I saw Bushwick on 59th and Paulina. He said, "Hey Smith, I told your punk ass that you didn't have shit on me", and then his friends began to laugh. I let Bushwick have his moment as I kept driving by.

All of a sudden I realized what Mad Max told me. "Never let these punks disrespect you." I circled the block and pulled the squad car right in front of Bushwick and his boys. I said, "What did you say to me chump?" He just stared at me as his boys walked away and I head butted Bushwick and said, "You better watch the way you talk to me you little bitch! Now get the fuck off this corner!" Bushwick spit on the ground and turned to walk away. I grabbed him by the throat and put his head on the ground and told him to lick up the spit. He just kept his mouth closed. I picked him up and hit him in the chest and got into the squad car and drove away.

Ignoring the Holy Spirit

A year and a half after my first felony arrest I had participated in dozens of speedy trials under the tutelage of guys like Mad Max and Frantic Frank. On my path to becoming the real police I realized that having respect on the street is everything. I also learned the importance of looking out for fellow officers and their families. I became overwhelmed by the amount of violence and hostility in the African-American community-my community, and to make matters worse I was assigned to one of the most dangerous districts in the city of Chicago. The only protection that I had was to be crazier than "the bad guys" on the street. The tools that I used to help me get crazy were fast women and good whiskey. That's how I became the real police. Nevertheless, becoming the real police took a toll on my physical health, but even worse it took a toll on my spiritual life. I became a good cop on the street, but it wasn't my call. The only way I was able to ignore my true call was by ignoring the Holy Spirit. In my view, survival meant stepping out on my own and becoming my own monster.

Stepping Out On My Own

I was working the second watch without a partner. In Chicago police language it is known as 10-99 unit. I was assigned to a domestic disturbance and they sent Frantic Frank to assist me. When I arrived a lady met me outside and told me that her boyfriend took her purse. He was standing right next to her and so I asked him if he could just give her back her purse. He said that he did not have it. Frantic Frank arrived a few minutes later and when the boyfriend saw him pull up he immediately went to his vehicle and returned the purse. I asked Frantic Frank if he knew the guy and he said that he had given the guy a few "speedy trials" over the years.

I approached the guy and asked him why he didn't give the purse back when I asked him to. He just stared at me. I said, "You can't talk now?" I took out my nightstick out and tapped my left hand softly with it and said, "When I ask you a question you better tell me the truth motherfucker."

I struck him dead in the kneecap, he fell to the ground and I got into the squad car and drove away.

Cop on the Edge

A few minutes later the dispatcher told me to respond to a disturbance on 59th and Paulina and she sent a female officer who was barely five feet and less than 120 pounds to assist me. When I arrived on the scene I saw a huge man banging on the door and another man lying on the ground bleeding. I knew that I couldn't handle this guy by myself or with the female officer. I asked for a mobile with Mad Max. I said, "Squad can I get a mobile with Mad Max." She said, "Go ahead with your mobile 714." I said, "Mad Max can you meet me at 59th and Paulina?" Mad Max replied, "En route." The female officer and I remained in our vehicles until Mad Max arrived. When he pulled up we exited our vehicles and asked the big weight lifting guy what happened.

He said, "You see what happened I just knocked his punk ass out." All of a sudden a lady comes out of the house and says that this man and her son had been arguing over some money. She told us that the big weight lifting guy hit her son in the head with a brick because he asked for his money. The mother said that she wanted him arrested. The man looked at us and said, "I want my money."

Mad Max asked the man to place his hands behind his back. The man said, "You can't arrest me. I came here for my money and this motherfucker didn't have it so I beat his ass." Mad Max looked at me and I got behind the bad guy and slipped on my brass knuckles. Mad Max said, "We can do this the easy way." The man pushed Mad Max and tried to run, but Mad Max grabbed him and I grabbed him around the neck and we wrestled him to the ground. He wouldn't put his hands behind his back and so I started hitting him in the head with my brass knuckles. I pounded him several times about his head and Mad Max took his knuckles and just twisted them into the "bad guy's" eye until he finally gave up.

We put the cuffs on him, searched him and then arrested him for battery. The man told us that he wanted to go to the hospital because he couldn't see. Mad Max said, "You should have thought about that before you put your hands on a police officer. You are lucky that I am in a good mood or else I would still be beating the living shit out of you!" Mad Max looked at me and said, "Can you believe this asshole? He puts his hands on the police and now he wants to go to hospital." Mad Max looked at the "bad guy" and said, "You can't have it both ways. You are either going to be a bad motherfucker or a pussy. Bad motherfucker's don't go to the hospital. They go to jail." We called for the wagon to transport him into the station because we were both working by ourselves. When we finished our tour of duty Mad Max said to me, "I like the way you handled that asshole." I said, "Thanks for helping me out bro!"

Jazzy J

I checked the assignment sheet for the next day and I saw that I was scheduled to work with Jazzy J. Jazzy J and I were in the police academy together. She is a fun loving and classy lady. Jazzy J worked as a Cook County sheriff's officer before she became a police officer. We got along well. When I checked the assignment sheet and saw that I would be working with her I was very pleased.

It was a cold winter night in Englewood and so the radio was pretty quiet. We drove through an alley around 61st and Carpenter and we saw a makeshift house. Someone got some wood and built a "little house" it even had heat and we could hear a television playing in the background. Jazzy J and I looked at each other and said, "Only in the Wood." We had received only one call that night, and it was a burglar alarm. My partner Jazzy J and I decided to pick us up some coffee so that we could stay awake. We exited our vehicle and started to cross the street to go to the store, and out of nowhere a car comes speeding and strikes Jazzy J sending her straight up in the air. The only thing that I saw was Jazzy J fall to the ground. I immediately notified the dispatcher and the ambulance that my partner had just been struck by a vehicle. We did not get any kind of description of the vehicle because the car blind-sided us and turned the corner. We never found out who struck Jazzy J, but by the grace of God she lived. She suffered a broken leg, but she was back to work within a year. That's how fast things can happen on the street.

"Mack Brown"

It was a nice summer midnight during the summer of 1993, when my partner Mack Brown and I were called to the 007th police station detention area (Lockup). Mack Brown was super laid back. He made sure to back other officers up, but he would rather ride around and look at the women than to run a license plate. Mack Brown had three women. He would always say that his women made sure that he was well dresses and well fed. Mack Brown's motto was the first and the sixteenth. Those are the paydays of each month for police officers. Every payday Mack Brown used to say that he should sit in the lockup for theft of services because he said the job was like taking candy from a baby.

The dispatcher notified us to go into the seventh district to see the desk sergeant. We were told that a prisoner had escaped from the detention area. They gave us the arrest report and told us to go by his last known address to ascertain his probable whereabouts. I asked my friend in lock up how in the world he escaped. But I would find out very quickly that some of these guys who get caught up in the criminal justice system know the tricks of their trade and are very crafty. My friend told me that he escaped through the window. The window was so small that I still cannot imagine how he managed to make his way out.

Mack Brown and I proceeded to the address that was on the arrest report. When we arrived I rang the doorbell and a young lady answered the door. I greeted her by saying that my name is Officer Smith and I am looking for a man who listed this house as his address. Before I could finish, she said, every time he escapes, "Yall come looking for me and ask me the same questions. "What kind of police keep letting that fool get away? Yall can kiss my ass" and then slammed the door in my face. And as soon as the door closed we see a man dressed in dark clothes and a doo rag running from the back of the house. I took off running after him and my partner Mack Brown was right behind me. I tackled the man in the back yard of an abandoned building and Mack Brown grabbed him by the wrist and told him to put his hands behind his back. I took out my brass knuckles and put them on and hit him right in the jaw. I told him that he better not ever run from the police. We got him to the squad car and drove him back to the seventh district and took him into the lock up.

When we were in the car Mack Brown said, "Where the fuck did you get those brass knuckles from?" I told him that Mad Max hooked me up. He said that he wanted a pair and I told him to ask Mad Max.

When we arrived in the seventh district, Mad Max was in the station processing an offender. He saw me come in with the offender who had escaped from the lock up and said, "Smith you are getting pretty good at this shit." I said, "That's a hell of a compliment coming from a man like you." He patted me on the back and said, "Keep up the good work." I said, "Thanks Mad Max."

When we got back into the squad car Mack Brown asked me if I was ready to take lunch. I said, "Cool." Mack Brown said, "Have you ever been to Williams Inn pizza?" I said, "No." Mack Brown said, "Williams Inn is about the only restaurant in the district that I will eat in." I told Mack Brown that I was willing to check it out. We pulled over to 57th and Ashland and got of the squad car. We walked to the door and rang the buzzer. A pretty chocolate sister buzzed us in and greeted us with a smile. She said, "How are you gentlemen doing? We replied, "Not bad and you?" She said, "I'm just fine. Who is this young fella you have with you Mack?" Mack said, "This is my boy Drew. He's cool." She said, "Do you want your usual?" Mack Brown said, "Fo show."

She sat us down and went to the back and returned with a cold beer in a frosty mug and gave it to Mack Brown. Mack Brown took a big swallow and said, "This is just what the doctor ordered. He said, "Bring my boy Drew one and bring us a large sausage and cheese pizza." Mack Brown said, "I asked Mad Max for a pair of those brass knuckles and he told me that he would work on it for me. I could sure use them for these clowns out here." When the pretty chocolate lady brought out the pizza it was nice and hot. It was one of the most delicious pizza's I had ever eaten. I said to Mack Brown, "This is some good pizza. I have never heard of Williams Inn." Mack Brown said, "Stick with your boy and I will show you the ropes." We left Williams Inn and went back to fighting crime until our shift was over.

Mad Max II

When I was checking off, Mad Max approached me and asked if I wanted to work with him tomorrow because his regular partner needed to take the day off. I was honored. I told Mad Max to get his rest because we are going to do some real police work tomorrow. Mad Max said, "Yea, we are!" I went home filled with excitement. I was looking forward to working with Mad Max because he taught me how to be the "real police."

When we got to roll-call the next day Mad Max said, "I have a tip on a few car thieves so we'll check it out after roll-call." Mad Max told me to get the keys and the radio and meet him in the parking lot. I picked up our equipment and gave Mad Max the keys. Mad Max drove over to 59th and Damen and put the squad car in park. He said, "A lady that lives on this block told me that a guy in the house next door to her has a different car everyday. She said that there are always people hanging out on the block. Let's just relax here for a moment." We were there for about 30 minutes when we observed a young man driving a blue Chevy with no plates going northbound on Damen from 59th street. Mad Max eased out and made a u turn. We pulled behind the vehicle and Mad Max turned on the lights. The driver did not pull over. He sped up and made a right onto 55th street. When he approached Ashland, he jumped out of the car and started running south on Ashland. Mad Max said, "Get him Smith, I'll be right behind you. I jumped out of the squad car and chased him down Ashland. He made a left on 56th street and I was right on his tail. I tackled him and placed the cuffs on him. After we ran the vehicle identification number we found out the vehicle was stolen. We took the bad guy in and found out that he had stolen two cars before, but he didn't do much time because he was a juvenile.

Mad Max had a knack for getting things done. It didn't matter what it was. From taking guns off the street, to catching an auto thief Mad Max got his share of the "bad guys". Mad Max was the "Real Police"!

Old School Charlie

I was working with Old School Charlie. Old School Charlie was about sixty years old. He worked the Halsted mall car. His job was to patrol the mall from 63rd to 65th on Halsted. If there was an easy job in Englewood this was it, but even the mall car got its share of crazy calls. One night Old School Charlie and I were eating Harold's fried chicken when we saw two women fighting. Harold's chicken is a Chicago favorite. It is not necessarily good for you, but it sure taste good. I said to Ole School, let's break this up. Ole School said, "Wait a minute. First of all I am still eating my chicken, and secondly there is nothing like seeing a good old fashion cat fight." When we got out of the squad car to break up the fight the women looked at us and said, "We just fucking around." Old School Charlie said, "Well you are going to have to fuck around somewhere else." One of the lady's said, "Why you so uptight officer, and then lifted up her skirt and said, "You want some of this pussy?" Old School Charlie said, "I wouldn't fuck you with a dead man's dick."

One night Old School Charlie pulled over on 64th and Lowe and said do you mind if we take a personal. I said that's cool with me. Old School Charlie said, "I will be right back." He returned about thirty minutes later. He looked at me and said, "It's rough in the Wood, but the pussy be good." Old School Charlie had just left one of his girlfriends' apartment and he had a huge smile on his face. We drove around for a minute and then found a hole. A hole is where an officer goes to get out of the public view to get a little rest. Old School Charlie and I both fell a sleep for a few hours. When we woke up Old School Charlie requested a radio check to see if we had been redlined. If the dispatcher calls you three times and you don't answer, you could be disciplined. He said, "Squad this is 706 Adam, can I get a radio check." The dispatcher said, "I read you loud and clear 706 Adam." By acknowledging us like this it was clear that the dispatcher was not trying to reach us and that we weren't redlined. Old School Charlie looked at me and said, "I love this job, and it damn sure beats working for a living."

I enjoyed Old School Charlie because he had been on the job for such a long time and he had some of the greatest stories to tell. He told me that an inspector approached him one night while he was sleeping in the squad car. The inspector knocked on the window and Old School Charlie looked at him. Old School Charlie motioned to the inspector to give him a second. Old School Charlie closed his eyes and then made the sign of the cross as if he were finishing a prayer and then he rolled down the window. The inspector looked at Ole School Charlie and just walked away.

Old School Charlie kept a shotgun in the car at all times. He would go to his personal vehicle right after roll car and put it in the trunk of the squad car. He said that if you are going to shoot a "motherfucker" you want to make sure he can feel it! I can see him now. Whenever he backed up other officers, he would pull out his shotgun to cover the subjects. They were just terrified at the sight of that shotgun. The older officers were fun to work with because they had all these great stories to tell but I got real used to the way Mad Max handled things on the street. I enjoyed it so much that I tried to pattern my way of doing things after his.

Bus Check Bill

When I first joined the Chicago Police Department we were on rotations. We would work 28 days on midnights, 28 days on days, and 28 days on the afternoon. After the midnight rotation we would have a watch party on the last tour of duty on midnights. The watch parties were excellent. We would have all sorts of food and drink and good music and we would eat, drink, dance, and tell stories. It was a wonderful time.

Bus check Bill was another old-timer that I enjoyed working with. Bus check Bill was in the KMA (Kiss my Ass) club. And he would always say that I'm in the KMA club whenever he was upset about something or someone on the job. The KMA club is for officers who have enough time on the job and are eligible for retirement. He was a good guy was a very easygoing. He worked the wagon and he did his job well, but at this point in his career he was not making very many arrests. Bus check Bill was a year away from retirement. He would always check off with at least five CTA checks and that's why we called him Bus check Bill. He used to say: "You are a good man Smith and there's not too many of us left."

Bus check Bill told me that he used to be like Mad Max and Frantic Frank when he was young, but he said that those days are long behind him. Bus check Bill said that he is buying a home in Florida and he is going to move there when he retires and that he never wants to see Englewood again.

Disco

I was working one summer day with my partner Disco. Disco likes house music and cigars. He is a cool easygoing dude. We received a call of a domestic battery. When we arrived on the scene we observed a very large man sitting on the steps of his house. He had a Jheri curl and he was wearing a lime green shirt and blue jeans. We informed him that we were called here. He replied very calmly that his wife called on him. He was very polite. He walked us into the house. He even asked us if we wanted anything to drink. We told him that we were cool. He took us to his wife. His wife wore a Jheri curl also and she stood about 5ft 2 and she was very heavy and then his wife proceeded to tell us what happened and said that she wanted him arrested for hitting her and then all of a sudden he became enraged.

So we said let's talk about it. We tried to talk to him because initially he seemed to be a very reasonable man, but he did not want to listen to us. His wife said, "I already told yall that I want him arrested because he hit me." Disco had the woman sign a complaint. We told her husband that we were going to have to take him into the seventh district police station for domestic battery. Disco said, "Sir please put your hands behind your back because your wife has signed complaints against you." He said, "You can go to hell because I am not leaving my house." I said, "Sir there is nothing we can do about it. You will have to deal with it in court." He told us to kiss his ass and to get the fuck out of his house.

When we attempted to put the handcuffs on him he refused to give us his wrists. I grabbed his arm and he threw me across the room and pushed Disco to the ground. I got on the radio and called for help. Then all of a sudden a young boy about fifteen years old ran towards me with a frying pan. He said, "Get your damn hands off of my daddy." I hit him right in the face and he fell to the ground. The man was choking Disco and so I jumped on his back and he began to spin me around the room, but just a few seconds later I heard the sirens and saw my fellow Englewood rangers come to our aid. Mad Max was the first one through the door. He ran toward the guy with his nightstick and shoved it right on his Adams apple. The man fell to the ground and started coughing. We placed the cuffs on him. After we had handcuffed him, his wife said that she changed her mind and did not want to press charges. But it was too late we already had the complaint signed.

I told Mad Max that I was sure glad to see him. He said, "Don't worry Smith, when an officer calls for help I will haul ass to get there. I see that you and Disco were handling your business." I said, "Yea, but as you can see this guy was hard to bring down." Mad Max said, "His fat ass is down now!"

We laughed, and then Mad Max asked me to come have a drink with him when our tour of duty was over. I met Mad Max at a policeman's bar that did not have any windows. When I got in there I saw a few of the guys from the seventh district and to my surprise Monster was there. Monster looked at me and said "Who told you about this place?" Mad Max walked up and said, "This is my boy Smith." Monster said I know him he was in six. Mad Max said, "Well he is an Englewood ranger now and he has been kicking a lot of ass and taking names." Monster looked at me and said, "Welcome to the police department." I said, "Thanks." Monster told the bartender to pour me a shot of Jack Daniels whiskey. The bartender said, "Are you sure you want that?" Mad Max said he is in the big leagues now and he can handle his shit!" The bartender brought me the Jack Daniels and I drank it straight down. She looked at me and said, "Damn, I guess you are in the big leagues." Mad Max said, "I told you so." Monster said, "I see you are all grown up now huh?" I said, "You damn right!"

Monster said, "You are ok Smith. I see those boys in Englewood have tightened up your game." I said I've been working with Mad Max. Monster, said, "That will do it. I know about Mad Max. That motherfucker is almost as bad as me!"

One-Rock Chris

One Rock Chris was a very interesting character. He liked to talk real loud and he enjoyed talking about everybody. He was in his mid-fifties and he loved to work out. One day we were in the station and One Rock Chris was talking to one of the female officers who worked behind the desk. When we left the station One Rock Chris said, "Did you see the way Candy was looking at my chest? She really wants some of One Rock Chris, but I aint giving her a damn thing, she is too old for me."

Candy had a lovely brown complexion and a beautiful personality. One Rock Chris could only dream about being with Candy, she wouldn't be caught dead with him. Candy was a part of crew, which called themselves the 3sb's (Thirty sector bitches) they regularly worked in the thirty sector. (Beats 731, 732,733, 734 and 735). The thirty sector borders were approximately 69th street on the north and 75th street on the south, and from the Dan Ryan on the East end and Hamilton on the West end. These women had three things in common. They were chocolate, beautiful, and they didn't take any shit!

One night, One Rock Chris asked me to work plain clothes with him because his partner got injured on the job. He said, "I hear you have been putting in some work out here in the Wood." I told him that Mad Max had been showing me the ins and outs. He said, "Mad Max don't take no shit! That's why I want you to work with me." I said sure, I didn't know what I was getting into and I thought that it would be cool to be in plain clothes and so I worked with One Rock for Chris about two weeks.

We were not on the street for more than five minutes when One Rock Chris picked up a prostitute and told her to go to the dope house and buy some crack. She said, "What are you going to do for me?" One Rock Chris said, "Bitch if you don't do what I say I am going to lock your funky ass up." She said, "I aint done nothing so you can kiss my ass." One Rock Chris said, "Do this for me and I will look out for you." She said that's more like it. One Rock Chris gave her ten dollars and we parked the unmarked car and followed the lady to the dope house. We hid behind the side of the door and when the lady bought the crack One Rock Chris grabbed a man who was only wearing a pair of green shorts and snatched him out of the house and wrestled him to the ground and we placed the handcuffs on him and arrested him. We recovered one clear plastic bag containing one rock of crack cocaine.

The prostitute asked One Rock Chris to give her something for helping him. One Rock Chris said, "Bitch, get your funky ass out of my face and just be glad that I didn't lock your nasty ass up, you funky ass cow!" She told One Rock Chris that she hoped that somebody would blow his damn head off and she ran down the street calling him every name in the book.

One Rock Chris told me that he didn't give a damn about these chicken heads in the street.

This is how One Rock Chris made many of his arrests by getting prostitutes to buy for him. One Rock Chris loved his job and he loved to talk a lot. He told me that he was working with Mad Max one day and they got into a high-speed chase. He said that Mad Max had hit three parked cars as they were chasing a guy wanted for armed robbery. The man jumped out of the car and started running and Mad Max fired about seven rounds at him but he didn't hit him. He said they chased him down and gave him one of the speediest trials ever. He said that Mad Max had blood all over his brass knuckles from going upside the dude's head. One Rock Chris said, "Mad Max is one crazy bastard and I love him!"

Sweet O

On a hot summer day in August my partner Sweet O and I were patrolling the streets when we heard the sound of gunfire around 55th and Halsted. Sweet O said, "Did you hear that?" I said, "Here we go". Some other officers had also heard the gunfire and notified the dispatcher. And as soon as the officer began to talk the dispatcher said, "Units in the seventh district we are getting a call of shots fired from a brown vehicle license plate unknown at 55th and Halsted." We toured the area looking for the offenders and as we turned onto Peoria street Sweet O said there they are. We saw a brown Chevy Monte Carlo speeding down Peoria street. One of the men turned around and when he saw us he threw a gun out of the passenger side window.

Sweet O got on the radio and said, "Squad we are right behind the vehicle and we are pulling it over at 57th and Peoria." Other officers arrived on the scene at which time Sweet O and I pulled the vehicle over. We took out our guns and slowly approached the car. We said put your hands out of the window so we can see them. I said, "If you make one crazy move I will blow your fucking head off." The offenders placed their hands out of the window and when we approached them I observed a semiautomatic handgun on the floor of the passenger side. I told the passenger to get out of the car and get on his knees. He got out of the vehicle and I struck him across the back with my nightstick and then placed the handcuffs on him. We recovered the firearm and took the offenders in for processing. They were eventually charged with Aggravated Battery and Unlawful Use of a Weapon. Mad Max and Frantic Frank were on the scene. Frantic frank said, "Smith you are really putting in some work." Mad Max said, "Are you trying to break my arrest record?"

Batman

I was working with Batman one night when he looked at me and said, "How do you like the job so far?" I told him that it was cool and that I have really learned a lot from working with Mad Max. Batman said, "Yea, Mad Max is a good officer. He kind of reminds me of myself because we don't take any shit of these sorry motherfuckers! You have to let them now who is the boss right away or they will try to run shit, but they don't run shit, but they got damn mouth and they better not talk to much because I will slap the living shit out of them." I told Batman that I understand and I am ready to kick ass whenever I need to. Batman said, "Have you ever served a warrant?" I said, "When I was in training in the sixth district I rode along to assist the tact team." Batman said, "Well I'm not talking about assisting, I'm talking about bringing the son of a bitch in on your own." I replied, "In that case no." Batman told me to follow him and he went into the station and gathered all of the warrants and said. "We are going to get us a bad guy tonight". Batman used to carry a sledgehammer with him to help him bust down the doors. We went over to little Mississippi, that's what we called one of the roughest areas in Englewood, which is on the northwest side of the district in the ten sector. Batman knocked on the door and a little boy about five years old let us in.

Batman asked the little boy if Jimmy Lee was in the house. The little boy pointed and said, "He is in the room with my momma." We approached the room with our guns drawn and saw Jimmy Lee having sex with the boy's momma. She saw us and began to scream. Jimmy Lee turned around and when he saw us he said, "Let me bust my nut since yall going to take me to jail". Batman said, "Get your black ashy ass up and don't try a damn thing because if you do, I am going to shoot that little dick of yours off and shove it down your throat." Jimmy Lee said, "Chill the fuck out, I can't do a damn thing to yall. I am butt ass naked."

Batman told me to put the cuffs on him. He did not resist when I placed the cuffs on him. He just asked if he could put his clothes on first. Batman told him that his woman would dress him. When I placed the cuffs on him we found his pants and had his woman put them on him and we took him out of the house and placed him in the rear seat of the squad car. When we were in the squad car Batman said, "Did you see the tits on his broad?" I said, "How in the hell could you miss them?" He told Jimmy Lee that he was going to go back and finish where he left off. Jimmy Lee told Batman to go fuck himself. We laughed all the way to the seventh district.

Batman told me that he was working one night and he pulled over behind the school on 74th street to get a little rest. When he went to the rear of the school, he saw a black car parked with the engine still running. He said, "I approached the car and I saw a couple in the back seat fucking like two rabbits. I stood there for about two minutes before they finally looked up. When they looked at me I flashed my light right on them and they started putting their clothes on." Batman said that they rolled down the window and apologized and he told them, "For what? I like watching naked movies." Batman said they drove off and he went to the rear of the school and got his rest.

Mc Crazy

Batman asked me if I knew the Mc Crazy family. I said, "I heard about them, but I have never been on a call there". The Mc Crazy family was well known in the seventh district. They had about fifteen children and the boys were always in trouble. Batman said when you hear a call at their address be sure to be ready to kick ass. Batman drove over to their address just to show me the house. When we got over there, there were a few of the brothers just hanging out. When they saw us drive by they just looked at us and spit on the ground. That's their way of showing disdain and a lack of respect for the police.

The Mc Crazy boys were known for being police fighters. Whenever the police were called to their house several officers would respond because they did not think twice about fighting the police even though they lost every time they squared off with an Englewood ranger.

Cat Murderer

I was working the second watch and after roll-call I went to the eight district to Dunkin' Donuts to get a glaze donut and a cup of coffee. After I scanned the Chicago Sun-times I patrolled the blocks on my beat. I looked over and saw a boy who looked to be about eight years old throwing a kitten against the side of a brick wall. It was if he was playing handball with the kitten. I got out of the squad car and approached the child. I said, "Son don't do that. You are hurting the kitten". He said I'm just playing with him. His mother came out of the house and said, "What's wrong Mr. Officer?" I said I was telling your son to stop throwing the kitten against the wall. She said, "Shit, I thought you were looking for one of these bad ass kids around here, but you talking a damn cat." And she went right back into the house. I told the boy to leave the cat alone and I got back into the squad car shaking my head in disbelief.

Damn Zombie

I was working the second watch (7am-3pm) and when my tour of duty was over that day I went to the Tiki room, one of my old watering holes and ordered a strong drink known as a zombie. After I finished it, I asked the bartender for another one, but he said that the policy is that you can only have one zombie a night because the alcohol content was so strong. I then ordered a hurricane and after I drank that I began to feel real mellow. All of a sudden Mack Brown came in with two beautiful women. He said, "What are you doing here all by yourself?" I told Mack Brown that I came here just to relax my mind. Mad Max said, "These are my girls Trina and Susan. I hang out with them whenever I relax my mind." We laughed and talked for a few hours and then left.

I went home and crashed out. I woke up the next day with a serious headache. My first call right out of roll-call the next morning was a "well being check." A woman called 911 because she had not seen her friend in a few days. I went to the location that the dispatcher had given me and I had to climb the steps to the top floor because the elevator was out. When I finally made it up the stairs, the engineer of the building let me into the man's apartment. I entered the room and observed the man lying on his bed. He was dead from an apparent head wound.

As I began to notify the dispatcher, I started to feel very hot and dizzy. I went into the dead man's bathroom and threw up. When the ambulance arrived they looked at me and wondered if I needed to go to the hospital. I told them that I would be fine. After I completed the paperwork I asked the lieutenant if I could be excused for the day, he was gracious and let me go home. I made it home at one o'clock in the afternoon. I was so tired and sick that I slept until five in the morning the next day.

Chapter 3

Erica

Erica

I went to work the next day and I was in a pretty good mood. I was working by myself and the sun was shining and the weather was about eighty degrees. It was nice and comfortable outside. As I was driving slowly patrolling my beat I saw one of the prettiest ladies I had ever seen wearing a powder blue blouse and some blue jean shorts standing on the corner of 58th and Loomis. She was about 5feet 3 and she wore her hair braided and had a lovely dark complexion. She did not have one blemish on her face. And even better, she had what the brothers like to call, a "big onion." In other words she had a nice and round rear end. I pulled the squad car over and asked her for her name. She said, "Why do you want to know? Am I in trouble?" I said, "Not at all, I just think you are one beautiful woman".

She said my name is Erica, and what is yours? I said my friends call me Drew. Erica said, "Don't you have something better to do than harass women on the street?" I told her that I would get back to work as soon as I got her telephone number. She gave me her number and said, "I know you are not going to call me, but it was nice meeting you." I told her that I was going to surprise her and then I drove away.

About a week later I responded to a street disturbance on 57th and Ashland. When I arrived on the scene Frantic Frank and Mad Max were talking. I went over and asked them about the disturbance and they said that when they arrived they did not see anyone. All of a sudden I hear a female voice calling my name. I turn around and it's Erica. Mad Max and Frantic Frank looked at me and smiled. Frantic Frank said, "Ole Smitty is really learning this job." I laughed and walked over to talk to Erica. She said, "I knew that I wasn't going to hear from you, I don't even know why I gave you my number." I told Erica that I was just getting out of a relationship and I just wanted to get my mind right. She said, "Well why the hell did you ask for my number?" I told her because she is so lovely. Erica looked at me and walked away.

I called Erica when I got home that evening. She told me that she couldn't believe that I actually called her. I asked her why she would say that and she replied that she gave a few police officers her number but they never called. She said that most guys just want to sleep with her but they don't want a commitment. She began to tell me that she dropped out of a small college down south after her first year because she missed Chicago, and she was looking for a job. We talked about many things.

Erica asked me if I liked being a police officer. I told her that it was a fun job but it could also be very dangerous at times. She said, "Did you ever shoot anybody?" I told her no, but I know several police officers that have. Erica replied, "I'm too wild to be a police officer because I would probably shoot a whole bunch of motherfuckers." We just laughed and she looked at me and gave me a hug.

Erica was twenty-three years old and she didn't have any children and she lived in a decent one-bedroom apartment in Englewood. She loved to drink vodka and cranberry juice and she smoked weed occasionally. I loved spending time with Erica because she loved to laugh and she was fun to be around. Erica and I became good friends and we did many things together. We were a real team. When Erica first came over to my apartment she started looking around. She said, "You need some pictures and flowers in here." She saw my degree sitting on top of my bookshelf and said, "So you graduated from Loyola?" I said, "Yes." She said, "What did you study?" I said, "Theology". Erica said, "Are you a preacher?" I said, "No." She said, "Then why in the hell did you study theology?"

I told Erica that I thought about becoming a priest. Erica looked at me and said, "Hell naw, you mean to tell me that you didn't want any pussy? You must have been smoking crack?" We both laughed. Erica saw a picture of Sabrina also on my bookshelf. She said, "Who is this?" I told her that it is a picture of my ex-girlfriend. Erica said, "If she is your ex you need to put that shit away in a box."

I told Erica that it's just a picture and Erica said, "You think I have some picture of some mother fucker that I used to date hanging on my wall? Old News goes in the garbage and that's where that bitch's picture should be!" Erica came to my apartment the next day and gave me a picture of her. She said, "Now you can just put that tramps picture away and put mine right here." I took Sabrina's picture and lit a match to it and flushed it down the toilet. Erica said, "Now that's more like it."

Erica was so much fun. She would come to my apartment and cook. She is an excellent cook and so we always ate well. I was never a card player but she taught me how to play spades and we would play spades and listen to music as a form of relaxation. One night Erica came over and fried some catfish. She told me to put on my old school music. I pulled out my Bobby Womack CD and played it for Erica. The song, *"A Woman's Gotta Have It"* was playing. She said, "You hear that baby?" A woman's gotta have it. You have t let me know that you need me around!" I said, "I feel you love." She said, "Now that's some real mellow music and that's just what I need." I said, "You sound a little stressed out." Erica said, "I'm just tired of the same old bullshit!" I said, "What do you mean?" Erica said, "I feel like my life is just passing me by." I said, "Well, what are you going to do about it?" Erica looked at me and smiled. Then she said, "Do you have any vodka?" I said, "I just have some brew and some Old number seven." Erica said, "Shit let me hit that Jack." I poured her some Old number seven and she began to fry the fish.

Erica made the best catfish. I said, "Baby this is some good eating. I really appreciate your friendship." Erica said, "I will do anything for you." We finished our meal and continued to listen to some music, and then all of a sudden Erica said, "Let's go to the Checkerboard." I said, "The joint in Englewood where the strippers dance?" Erica said, "Hell yea!" We went to the club and I saw a few of my fellow officers in there.

The dancers were grooving to Tupac. I ordered a shot of Jack Daniels and Erica ordered absolute vodka and cranberry juice. I said, "You have been drinking Jack Daniels. Are you sure that you want to switch up your drinks?" Erica said, "I'm a bad ass bitch from the Wood, now get your baby some vodka!" I said, "Cool." As the girls were dancing, Erica began to do a strip dance of her own. I found it quite fascinating, as did my fellow officers. Erica jumped up on the stage and started dancing. One of my fellow officers went over to Erica and tried to touch her. Erica said, "You can stop right there, all of this belongs to my man." Erica looked at me and smiled. Erica helped me to get over my relationship with Sabrina but I had a friend who was not so lucky.

Billy Boy

Billy Boy was a nice guy who I had met when we were younger. He worked in the 18th district where a lot of the nice nightclubs are. In the eighteenth district you see people bar hopping at 1 and 2 in the morning. The only reason that a citizen may approach you is to get directions to one of the happening clubs. Billy Boy would never be caught in any hole in the wall club in Englewood. He dressed like a preppie; he liked the polo shirts and the penny loafer shoes. He was a nice guy and he loved the ladies. He had several women but he had one that he just couldn't get over. She broke up with him and told him that she would never see him again. Billy Boy did not give up. He kept on trying to win the woman back. Nevertheless, she refused. She told Billy Boy to move on with his life. One day I received a call from a fellow officer who told me that Billy boy went to the lakefront and shot himself in the chest. I couldn't believe it. I was devastated. I knew that he was hurting, but I didn't know that he was considering suicide.

I talked to a mutual friend of ours about the incident and he said, "I didn't know Billy Boy was that weak." I replied, "I wouldn't say that he was weak. He was just in so much pain and he didn't know where to turn to for help." I went to the funeral with Mack Brown and we overheard one of the female officers say to another female officer, "Damn I would have given him some "pussy." Mack Brown said, "I wish Billy Boy would have talked to me because I would have told him that pussy aint nothing but recreation."

After we left the funeral Mack Brown told me that he has three women because you have to always let the women know that you have other options. I told Mack Brown that Billy Boy had a couple of other women, but Mack Brown said, "Yea, he did, but the mistake he made was getting pussy-whipped. My broads know that they can easily be replaced."

I said, "Mack, the brother must have been going through a great amount of pain". Mack Brown said, "I liked Billy Boy, but aint no pussy worth a motherfucker dying for!" Pussy is just entertainment and when you begin to believe otherwise you become a square ready to be played. Billy boy was a payer, but ole Mack Brown is a player."

Mack Brown asked me how Erica was doing. I told Mack Brown that Erica is down for me. He said, "That's good, but you better stay in control and keep your player game tight because I don't want you to end up like Billy Boy." I told Mack Brown that I have my game together, but I really feel for Billy Boy and his family.

Erica II

I took Erica to the Wisconsin Dells for her birthday and we partied for three days. We went on the water slides and took some photos. I got back in town a little late and I had to go right to work. I was a little tired so I asked the lieutenant if I could take a few hours on the front and come in two hours later than the original starting time. He granted me the time and so I took Erica home and chilled at her crib for a few hours before I went to work. As soon as I got there Mad Max picked me up and we responded to a call of a homicide. When we got to the house there were three men lying dead. One was slumped across a chair, and another was on the couch face down, and one was lying on the kitchen floor. I looked at Mad Max and said, "What the hell happened here?" Mad Max got on the radio and called the crime lab to come out and process the scene. Mad Max said, "I believe this is a dope hit. We always receive calls here about somebody selling dope." Mad Max looked at one of the dead men and said, "This is Gangster Pete, and they finally got his ass." Gangster Pete was a known drug dealer but on this night his days of slinging dope came to an end.

Dead on the Tracks

It was a nice sunny day and Sweet O and I were patrolling the street on a relatively quiet day when we responded to a call of a death investigation on the Chicago Transit Authority train tracks at 63rd and Halsted. Sweet O is an excellent police officer. She has a real good sense of the streets and she is a tremendous report writer. Sweet O never chased anyone. She said, I don't need to run because Motorola can catch the fastest son of a bitch in the world."

When we arrived at 63rd and Halsted we walked up the stairs and we observed an 11-year-old boy dead on the tracks. The Chicago Fire Department picked the child up and placed him in an ambulance. He was killed because he had been playing on the train tracks and he stepped on the third rail and was electrocuted to death. Now mind you, I had witnessed many tragedies and have seen several killings on the street, but the death of this young boy really affected me, and when his mother arrived on the scene her grief brought tears to my eyes. Sweet O and I filled out the necessary paperwork but afterwards we were in our own state of mourning. It made us reflect upon how fragile life really is. I felt for the family, but what can you say to someone in the midst of such a terrible tragedy?

We went to St. Bernard Hospital to complete the hospitalization case report. As we were talking to the mother we could hear the pain and grief in her voice as she fought back the tears. When we finished getting the necessary information for the case report, we both gave the mother a hug. There was nothing that we could say. We just left the hospital in sadness.

We left the hospital and Sweet O said, "Squad beat 723 is up and clear. And then we heard a call come from the dispatcher. "Beat 723, take a theft in progress at 66th and Morgan." Sweet O responded, "10-4 squad." As we approached the location we saw a man dressed in all blue running down the street. Sweet O got on the radio and said, "Squad, do you have a description of the offender?" The dispatcher said, "He is a male Black about 6feet even wearing a blue shirt and blue jeans." Sweet O replied, "We see a man fitting that description running northbound up Morgan." I pulled alongside of him on 65th and Morgan. I put the car in park and took off after him. It only took me a few strides to catch up with him. I tackled him to the ground at which time I heard the dispatcher say that the offender snatched 200 dollars out of a woman's hand while she was at the Currency Exchange. The man didn't resist arrest or fight back. He said that the money was in his right pocket and that he took the money to feed his family. I recovered the money and we went back to the Currency exchange and returned the woman's money to her.

Summer Time with Jim-Jim

In the summer of 1996 I applied to work the summer mobile unit. I figured that this would be an excellent time for me to relax and get away from the streets of Englewood. I was correct. The summer mobile unit patrolled Chicago's lakefront and for the most part it was fun. We would write citations for drinking and parking tickets, but we did not respond to many violent crimes. One day my partner Jim Jim and I were walking along the lakefront on the North side a lady approached us and said, officers could you help me. We said of course Miss, and she responded, "As I was walking some man gave me a menacing look." Jim Jim and I looked at each other and did our best not to laugh. I thought to myself, I could get use to this.

Jim Jim had been on the job for about eleven years and he had worked in many different districts and units. He was detailed to the summer mobile unit but he was assigned to prostitution. We were talking about this incident and we both had never had anyone approach us with "the menacing look" call. We both appreciated the change.

Nevertheless, on a summer day in June, people were in the park barbecuing and playing soccer and softball. Jim Jim and I were patrolling the lakefront when a woman approached us and said that a man wearing a red sweat suit and black Kangol hat ran up behind her and snatched her purse. She said that he was with a man in a white tee shirt and blue jeans. Jim Jim and I toured the area when we spotted them walking in the park. We got out of the squad car and began to walk slowly toward them. The man in the red sweat suit turned around and saw us and then they took off running. Jim Jim said you get the one in the white tee shirt and I'll get the guy in the red.

We took off after them and as we were running through the park people were screaming and shouting. You could hear them saying, "Oh my God what is going on? I tackled the guy in the white tee shirt and Jim Jim tackled the guy in the red and minutes later we retrieved the woman's belongings. When we got back in the squad car Jim Jim said, "Man I did not come to summer mobile for this shit!" I replied, "I feel you my brother!"

The next day Jim Jim and I were working the South side of the Lakefront. We were sitting in the squad car doing some people watching and all of a sudden we hear shots fired and we see two men running from the beach at 79thstreet. Jim Jim notified the dispatcher, "Squad, we just heard shots fired around 79th and the lakefront." We took off after them in the squad car. But we never caught up with them.

Erica and Laura

When summer mobile ended in the fall, we had a huge police party on the twelfth street beach. We had plenty of food and drink. We had wonderful music and it was just a relaxing time. I was dancing with Erica. Erica had on a blue two-piece bikini swimsuit. I looked up to heaven and understood what my father meant when he says, "If God created anything better than woman, God kept it to Himself." All of a sudden I look to my left and Lovely Laura walks over to me and says, "How is my favorite little man? I told you that we would meet again." I said, "Hey Lovely Laura; it's good to see you. This is my friend Erica." Lovely Laura looked at Erica but did not say a word. She looked at me and said that she would be calling me soon. She looked Erica up and down and walked away. Erica said, "Who is that?" I told her that she is a police officer in the sixth district. Erica said,

"Are you fucking her?" I said, "No" and she replied, "I don't care if that bitch is the police I will beat her ass."

I told Erica that she didn't have to be concerned with Lovely Laura because she was real cool and besides she is dating this crazy ass policeman and I don't want to have anything to do with him. Erica said, "I really like you and I don't want to lose you". I told Erica that I am down for her. We danced and partied all night along the beach. I ran into some friends of mine from the police academy. I even saw Monster from a distance but I did not approach him.

Lovely Laura called me the next day and told me to come over. I told Lovely Laura that I wouldn't be comfortable at her house but she was more than welcome to come see me. Lovely Laura came over to my apartment with a bottle of Moet champagne. I said, "What's the special occasion?" She said, "I'm the special occasion". Lovely Laura was wearing a red dress with some red high heel shoes. I told her to come in and make herself at home. I popped opened the champagne and poured us each a glass. Lovely Laura came and sat down next to me on the couch. She said, "So, who is that girl you were dancing with last night? I said that it was my new woman Erica. Lovely Laura said, "That's so cute." She got closer to me and said, "So, you don't want any of this?" I told Lovely Laura that I didn't want any part of Monster. She said, "I told you not to worry about him. I have him wrapped around my finger." I replied, but I don't' want my face wrapped around his fist.

Lovely Laura placed her hand on my thigh and said, "Don't you worry about a thing, mommas going to take care of you." My heart was racing with excitement. Lovely Laura was looking good and smelling even better. I just wanted to reach out and hug her, but I kept my cool. She kissed me in the lips and said, "Your woman is just a little girl but I'm a grown woman." I was speechless. She said, "Drink some more champagne because you need to loosen up." I drank some more champagne and Lovely Laura and I just began to talk. She said, "You really like that girl." I told her that we have a lot of fun together. Lovely Laura said, "Well I'm happy for you." Again I asked her about Monster. She said, "Monster is cool because he takes care of me. I am not going to interfere with your little girlfriend, but I know that you need some excitement." I told Lovely Laura that my whole life is excitement. She smiled as she poured us some more champagne. Lovely Laura said, "You aint had no excitement until you have experienced my passion." When Lovely Laura left the next day, I said to myself, "Damn! I know why Monster is crazy about her".

Fashion Fred

I returned to the seventh district in the fall after my detail to the summer mobile unit. I worked with Fashion Fred. Fashion Fred wore a lot of the latest styles. He loved his clothes and he loved to work out. He was a cool guy and a lot of fun. Fashion Fred said, "Since you are just coming back from that vacation at summer mobile, I know you are ready for some action." I asked Fashion Fred if there was anything that I missed while I was in summer mobile. Fashion Fred said, "You missed the same old shit; assaults, batteries, shootings, killings, robberies and whatever else is fucked up. How could you leave us for summer mobile?" We looked at each other and laughed. I told Fashion Fred that I am refreshed and ready to kick ass. He said, "You know Mad Max got another department commendation for catching an armed robber?" I told him that Mad Max is one bad dude. Fashion Fred said, "Hell yea, that cat aint no fucking joke!"

We responded to a call of shots fired on 68th and Winchester. When we arrived on the scene Fashion Fred and I saw two men running down the alley. We pulled out our guns and began to chase them. We heard gunfire and then we saw Mad Max and Frantic Frank apprehend the offenders. They recovered two semi-automatic handguns from the offenders. I went up to Mad Max and Frantic Frank and said, "You boys haven't lost a step." They said, "Welcome back Smith, we need you out here." I told them that I was back and I'm ready to rock and roll.

Fashion Fred and I responded to a gang fight on 71st and Damen. When we arrived on the scene there were people screaming and crying. We heard the sirens of our fellow officers' squad cars and an ambulance. We began pushing and shoving our way through the crowd. When we finally made it we saw two men lying on the ground bleeding. A lady was kneeling next to one of the men crying. She said, "They killed my baby, they killed my baby!" We began moving the crowd back in order to protect the crime scene, but it was so difficult because of the anger and chaos of the moment.

Chapter 4

Life in the Third District

Back on the block

In 1998, after seven years as an Englewood Ranger I transferred to the 003rd district because I was having some problems with a few thugs on my block. I lived in the district and so I knew that I would be able to handle the situation. The third district is a pretty fast district but it is not as fast as Englewood.

I told Mad Max that I was transferring to the third district because there were some chumps hanging on my block selling drugs and making all kinds of noise. Mad Max said, "Well we are going to miss you here, but I know you have to do what you have to do. I know that block will be quiet real soon when you start patrolling that beat." Mad Max and I just laughed. I told him that I was going to the third district to kick ass and take names.

I walked into the third district station to begin my first day as a third district officer. I walked into the watch commander's office and introduced myself to the watch commander. I said, "Hello Captain, my name is Andrew Smith I just transferred here from the seventh district." He said, "Welcome officer Smith, I'm Captain Law and I am the watch commander for the third watch. I was looking at your file and we are glad to have a fine officer such as yourself working with us."

Kid Joe

Captain Law told me that the roll-call room was just around the corner. I was working with Kid Joe. Kid Joe was about 6 feett 3 and had about eighteen months on the job. He was a nice guy, but he was a bit goofy to me. He thought he was a real tough guy and he thought he knew everything. Nevertheless, Kid Joe turned out to be a good man. I was new to the district and I didn't know many of the officers. After roll-call Kid Joe approached me and said, "Are you Smith?" I said, "Yes." He said, "I'm Kid Joe. Do you mind if I drive?" I said, "Cool." We got our radios and went to get the squad car.

Kid Joe was bragging about the arrest he made and then he looked at me and said, "Smith how do you like the job so far?" I said, "It's been good to me." He said, "Have you made any arrest?" I said, "I have made hundreds of arrest." He just laughed. I didn't say a word. He said, "Well you will learn how to be the police when you work with me." And I said, "Really?" He said, "Yea, I been out here for almost two years and I have made almost any arrest you can think of." He said, "So who is your Field-Training officer?" I said, "Do you mean who was my field-training officer?" He said, "What happened?" I replied, "Nothing." He said, "Well who is training you?" I said, "Son, I'm training your ass! I transferred from Englewood. I am an eight-year veteran and I have seen shit that will make you cry!" Kid Joe looked at me with his mouth wide opened and then he said, "What are you doing with all that time on the job?" I shouted, "Kicking ass and taking names so don't tell me about your little bullshit arrests. I aint no fucking rookie and so I'm not impressed. As a matter of fact pull over and give me the got damn keys." Kid Joe pulled over gave me the keys and apologized. I said, "Kid Joe; you have a lot to learn. The first thing that you need to know is that you should talk with your nightstick and numbers of arrest. I don't want to hear you bragging about being the police. I'm the damn police!"

Kid Joe and I responded to a call of shots fired and a theft in progress at 73rd and Rhodes. When we arrived on the scene we observed two men with red baseball caps exiting the vehicle described by the dispatcher. As we approached them they began to run. We chased them and caught up with them as they entered a basement apartment. The offenders locked the door on us but we kicked the door open and we gained entrance into the apartment and recovered a stolen computer, after further investigation we learned that the offenders had also stolen a vehicle. We took them into custody and charges were eventually approved for Possession of a Stolen Motor Vehicle.

I was glad that the day was over because Kid Joe really got on my last nerve. All he did was ask me questions about Englewood. When I left work that night I went to the bar with no windows, the one that Mad Max turned me on to and had a few shots of Jack Daniels. This was a regular routine of mine. I wasn't doing this because I was depressed I was enjoying myself. I ran into Mad Max and told him about Kid Joe. He said, "What did the guy's face look like when he found out you were a veteran from Englewood?" I said, "Pitiful." Mad Max laughed his ass off!

Rookie Barbara

I was working with a rookie officer by the name of Rookie Barbara. Rookie Barbara had just finished her eight-week field training and so she worked with different officers until she completed her one-year on the job and was no longer on probation. Rookie Barbara was a very kind and gentlewoman. She stood about 5feet 4 and wore a short hairstyle that was always nicely done. She had a smooth beautiful brown complexion. She was a single mother of a 15-year-old boy. Rookie Barbara didn't know too much about the streets, but she was willing to learn.

We received a call of a man selling drugs. When we arrived on the scene I spoke to the owner of the building and he said that this man is selling drugs in the doorway of his building. The "bad guy" said "You can search me; I do not have anything on me." I searched him and had my partner search the area of the building but we didn't find anything on him or in the area. I asked the man what was he doing in this building. The man said that he was just here visiting a friend. I asked him where is his friend and he told me that he is not here. I said, "Sir you have to leave". He said, "I'm not going anywhere I am going to wait for my friend."

I asked the owner of the building if he would sign a complaint for trespassing. The owner of the building said that he would sign the complaint. I asked the man once again to leave and when he didn't I attempted to place the handcuffs on him. He told me, "Get your fucking hands off of me." Rookie Barbara came to assist me and he pushed her to the floor. I took out my nightstick and struck him right in the head, and we began fighting and we ended up outside on the sidewalk and Rookie Barbara got on the radio and called for help. I was hitting him with my nightstick and all of a sudden blood started oozing from his forehead and he began to fight more aggressively.

Other officers arrive on the scene. Kid Joe tackled him and they begin rolling around on the street. I jumped in and grabbed his arm and was able to get one of his wrists handcuffed. He kept on fighting us and so I pulled the one cuff that I had on him as tight as I could until his wrist started bleeding and then he allowed us to handcuff him. We got him up on his feet and I told him that it didn't have to be this way and then I head butted him and put him in the back seat of the squad car. I heard someone from the crowd that was watching say, "That's why they are shooting the police, because yall aint shit!" They did not see me pleading with the guy inside the building or him refusing to cooperate and they didn't see him push an officer to the ground. They just saw a man getting beat up by the police.

Rookie Barbara was a little shaken up by the incident. She asked me how often I have gotten into fights as a police officer. I told Rookie Barbara that this is the line of work that she has chosen and so she better get used to it. I said fighting is synonymous with being the police. You are going to have to put your hands on these motherfuckers so they can understand you! She didn't say anything for a while. She just stared out of the window; at that point I began to reflect on my early days on the job and working with Monster and Mad Max. I said, "Barbara, there will be days when you are going to have to get physical out here, but don't worry about it because your fellow police officers will back you up."

When our tour of duty had ended, Kid Joe approached me and told me that a few of the guys would be in the parking lot slamming a few beers and that I should come and have a few with them. I joined a few of the other officers in the rear of the parking lot and we began to talk. One of the officers said, "Man, Kid Joe told us that you were a serious police officer." I told them that I was an Englewood ranger and you have no choice but to be tough. They asked me why I transferred to the third district and I told them that I live in the district and I needed to deal with some gangbangers who were constantly loitering around my crib.

They asked where I lived and when I told them they said, "Yea we get calls over there a lot." I said that I transferred to the third district so that I could put a stop to this madness. Kid Joe said, "We will help you clean up your block." I told Kid Joe that I appreciate his help and that I know it will be easy to do.

Kid Joe II

The next day I was working with Kid Joe and I drove to my block to see if the thugs were out their loitering. When we arrived we got out of the vehicle and I approached one of the guys known as Psycho. He looked at me in astonishment because he knew my face but he didn't know that

I was a police officer. I told Psycho that he was going to have to move his operation off of this block. He said, "I'm not doing anything. I'm just out here cooling out." I said, "I know you are selling drugs out here and it's going to stop. I am asking you nicely to clear out of here, but if I have to ask you again you will know that I mean business."

Kid Joe and I got back into the squad car and went back to patrolling our beat. I drove back to my block a few hours later and saw Psycho standing in the same place, as he was earlier. He looked at me and started to walk away. We got out of the squad car and I told Psycho to come over to me. He came over to me and I placed him against the squad car and began to search him. I told Kid Joe to look around the fence to see if he could find anything. Kid Joe didn't find anything and I didn't find anything on him and so I told him to clear out. Psycho began to walk away when the dispatcher said, "What unit is near 61st and Cottage Grove?" I said, "Squad beat 312 is." She said, "Are you guys alone?" I replied, "We are now." She asked us to get in the vehicle because she had received some information from a citizen. We entered the vehicle and the dispatcher said, "A citizen who wants to remain anonymous says that the man you guys just let go is selling drugs and he hides them in a pole on the fence." I said, "10-4 squad." Kid Joe went over to the fence and I began to walk towards Psycho. When he saw Kid Joe pull out a bag from inside the pole of the fence he took off running.

I took off right behind him. Kid Joe jumped in the squad car and followed us. Psycho was running westbound from 61st and Cottage. He went through someone's back yard and over a fence. I could hear Kid Joe on the radio, "Squad my partner is chasing a male black about 5ft. 9 westbound on 61st and Cottage." I jumped over the fence and I tackled him. I told Kid Joe that I had him in the back yard of 62nd and Cottage. Kid Joe arrived and saw me wrestling with Psycho. He jumped in and grabbed his arm. I reached in my pocket and took out my brass knuckles and hit Psycho right in the jaw and then we placed the cuffs on him. I told him that he should have believed me when I told him to take his operation somewhere else.

Kid Joe was excited. He said, "Man you are one crazy little motherfucker! That's how they do it in the Wood huh?" I said, "Kid Joe, I might laugh, smoke, and drink my Jack without coke but I aint no joke!" Psycho was in the back of the squad car screaming, "I'm going to sue your ass for hitting me in the jaw with those damn brass knuckles!" I told Psycho that I tried to talk to him like a gentleman but he didn't understand and therefore I had to speak to him in a language that I knew he could comprehend.

Rookie Barbara II

On a hot summer day in June of 1999 I was working with Rookie Barbara and we responded to a call of a man holding a gun to a woman's head. When we arrived the woman told us that her boyfriend placed a gun to her head and said that he was going to kill her. I asked the woman to give us a description of him. She told us that he had on a red baseball cap a white tee shirt and some blue jeans and that he is driving an old blue Chevy Impala. We began to search the area and observed the offender sitting in the car that his girlfriend described for us. Rookie Barbara was about to get on the radio but I told her to wait a minute because the guy was alone and I could handle him. I looked at Rookie Barbara and told her to relax. I could sense that she was extremely nervous. I told her to pull out her gun and ease up on the passenger side and that I would approach the drivers side.

We cautiously approached him with our weapons drawn. I shouted, "Put your hands where I can see them and if you make one crazy move I will blow your fucking brains out!" The offender showed us his hands and said, "What did I do officer?" I told him to put his hands on his head. He was moving slow and looking very nervous. I told rookie Barbara to point her gun right at his head. I holstered my gun and I pulled him from the vehicle and placed him in handcuffs. When I searched his car I recovered a loaded handgun and a large amount of marijuana from under the front seat of his car.

Rookie Barbara looked so relaxed when we were on our way into the station to process the offender. I asked her how she felt. She said, "My heart was beating like crazy, but I am fine now." I told Rookie Barbara that she did a fine job and that she would eventually get used to situations like this.

Felony C

I had been on the job for a while but I was in a different district and so I did not know many of the officers. I checked the daily assignment sheets and saw that I would be working with Felony C the next day. I knew that it was a reason why he was called felony C, but I didn't know what that reason was. I asked my friend and fellow officer Crazy eight ball Ashford why they called him that. He said because one day Felony C received a call of shoplifting from Walgreen's. When Felony C arrived on the scene, he observed a man running down the street with a forty-ounce bottle of beer. Felony C chased the guy down the street, through an alley and jumped over the fence and broke his foot. His partner caught the guy and they arrested him for a misdemeanor. Henceforth, he is known as Felony C this very day. I still can't believe Felony C almost killed himself chasing a man for stealing a beer.

When we got out of roll-call Felony C said, "So you are Smith?" I quoted the rapper Snoop Dog saying, "He is I and I is he." Felony C said, "Man I heard a lot about you. You are from Englewood huh?" I said, "Yes." He said, "Well I think you are going to like it here in the third district." I told Felony C that I agreed with his assessment. Felony C was in his early forties and he had about two years on the job. He wore his uniform pants real tight and he would always talk about how much he loved his girlfriend. I thought that was honorable and I respected him for that, but I thought to myself that Mack Brown would really talk bad about Felony C if he kept telling him how much he loved his woman.

Chapter 5

The hazards of being off duty

The purse

When you are a police officer you are on duty 24 hours a day. I never looked for any trouble when I got off of work and I was definitely not trying to be a super hero or super cop, but things just seemed to happen to me on a regular basis.

I was off duty one sunny day and I got on the bus to go downtown. I flagged down the 6 Jeffery and climbed the stairs. I showed the bus operator my police star and he let me on. (Free of charge) When the bus pulled over at Jackson and Michigan a man snatched a woman's purse and ran off the bus. I grabbed him, but he shook loose from me and so I ran after him. I chased him west bound down Jackson. I tripped and fell down and busted my chin and scratched up my leg and the man got away. During the foot chase he dropped the woman's purse and I was able to recover it and return it to the woman. I said to myself I will never do that again, but I was wrong! It seems as if I would get into the strangest altercations while I was off duty. I don't know if it was because I was developing a short temper from being in such hostile situations or if I was just at the wrong place at the wrong time. This was the first off duty incident that I was involved in, but it would not be the last.

Sabrina

I was on my way to a club to listen to some music with my girlfriend Sabrina. I met Sabrina during my last year at Loyola University and she was in her first year. Sabrina was from a northern suburb of Chicago. She was a very outspoken person and very cunning. She knew how to get whatever she wanted, and she did this by associating with certain people in the "know."

We had a pretty good relationship for the first few years but after a few years on the police department things began to get shaky. Sabrina started dating a professional football player and she told me that it was my fault because all I did was hang out with my fraternity brothers and other police officers. She eventually married a professional basketball player and told all of my friends that I was the bad guy and it was my fault that our relationship ended.

I was about to park my vehicle so that Sabrina and I could get something to eat and all of a sudden some guy pulls his car right into the parking space that I was waiting for and he just stared at me. I pulled my car next to his blocking him in. He exited his car from the passenger door and approached me. I reached into my pocket and pulled out my brass knuckles that I got from Mad Max and put them on. I said, "Didn't you see me with my signal on ready to park?" He said, "Fuck you!" I exited my vehicle and he swung at me. I hit him in the eye with the brass knuckles and the guy fell in the street and I jumped into my vehicle and drove off. Sabrina said, "What is wrong with you?" I said, "You don't know what its like on the street. You expect me to just let some chump disrespect me." She said, "Take me home that was totally uncalled for. You should have just found another place to park." I told Sabrina that I don't know how they do it in the suburbs, but I'm from Woodlawn! I drove her home and went out on the town to kick up some dust.

The next morning I received a phone call from Sabrina, and she asked me to come over to her apartment. I went over to Sabrina's place and she let me into her apartment. She took me into the kitchen and said this is Joe Pro Football player. I shook his hand and then I looked at Sabrina. I was confused. I didn't understand why she wanted me to meet this guy. I looked at her and said I have to leave. Sabrina called me a few hours later and told me that Joe Pro Football player is her new man and that our relationship was over. I was so hurt and angry that I couldn't say anything. I hung up the phone and went over to Sabrina's house. When she didn't let me in I kicked the door. I kept on kicking it until I broke the lock on the door. She called the police on me but I was gone. She got a complaint register on me and I received five days off without pay.

Sabrina called me and told me that she didn't want to call the police on me, but she had to because I broke her lock. I said, "Why would you invite me to your place when you have company?" She said, "I don't know, but please don't call me again because I am dating Joe Pro." I said, "You called me." Sabrina hung up the phone. The next time I saw her again she was married to a professional basketball player. I said, "I see you finally landed your professional athlete. Can you pay me back the five thousand dollars I loaned you for your tuition? She said, "That's what it costs to hang out with me." We both laughed and I haven't seen Sabrina since then.

Get the fu*k out of my face

I was leaving Happy's liquor store on 79th and Cottage Grove when a man about 30 years old, dressed in a blue sweat suit approached me and asked if I could spare some change. I didn't say anything I just kept walking. I'm thinking to myself that this dude is perfectly healthy. I work hard for my money and I refuse to give it to him. He followed behind me and said, "I asked you a question bitch." I said, "Get the fuck out of my face!" and then he pulled out a knife and said, "Give me your damn money or I'll cut your fucking throat!" I reached in my holster and pulled out my nine (barreta handgun) and pointed it at his face. He was startled; he slowly lowered his knife and stared at me with his mouth hanging open. I told him that I was giving him one second to get the hell out of my face and then I am going to start shooting. He took off running east on 79th and the guys standing on the corner just laughed their asses off. I went to Erica's house and drank my whiskey in peace. I told Erica about it and she fell out laughing. She said, "Let's go back there and see if his ass is still on the corner." I told Erica that I just wanted to cool out. She put on The Isley Brothers and we just mellowed out.

Tire Jacker

There are always things happening on the streets and so in a sense a police officer is always on duty because a crime can take place right in front of you and your instincts tell you to act. I happened to be looking at of my window one night when I observed a man attempting to steal my tire from under my 1994 Ford Explorer. I grabbed my revolver and ran down the steps. I opened the door and came out with my gun in my hand. A lady that was with him began to scream. She yelled, "Look out he has a gun." The man was startled. He looked up at me and before he could say anything, I put my revolver to his head and told him that I would blow his brains out. He started crying and pleading, "Please don't kill me! I'm sorry! Please sir! Please." I removed my revolver from his head and told him if he ever came around here fucking with my car that he could be assured that I would shoot him in his fucking balls. I told him to get up and get the hell out of here. He jumped in his car and he drove away with tears in his eyes.

I went back upstairs and put on some Stevie Wonder and began to relax. Erica called me and I told her what had just happened. I could hear the excitement in her voice. She asked me so many questions about the incident. She wondered if I knew the guy, or if he was with anybody. She asked if I used the nine or my revolver. She said, "You should have shot his punk ass." I just laughed and told her that he knows better than to fuck with me again. Erica, said, "Shit, I wish I was there with you." She asked me to come and get her so we could hang out.

I went to Erica's and blew the horn for her to come downstairs. Erica came down with some CD's in her hand. She got into the car and said, "Hey baby." I said, "What's happening". Erica said, "Let's go kick up some dust." She handed me a CD and said, "Rock this shit, this is my boy." I put in the CD and it was Tupac's song "How do you want it." Erica started singing and moving to the beat. She said, "I feel like dancing." I said, "Well where do you want to go?" She looked at me and said, "Let's do something different." I looked at Erica and I told her that I know exactly where we are going. I drove up to the North side of Chicago to the Red Hair Piano bar.

I valet the Ford Explorer and we went inside. Erica, said, "This is some cool and mellow shit." We found two seats at the bar, and the bartender approached us and asked what we wanted to drink. Erica said, "Let me get some vodka and cranberry juice," and I said, "Jack straight and an Amstel light." Erica said, "Where did you find this place?" I told her that one of my boys turned me on to it. She said, "This is really cool, my man gets around." She kissed me on the lips and said, "I love my baby!"

Erica asked the piano player if he could play her some Aretha Franklin. The piano player asked her what Aretha Franklin song she had in mind. Erica said, "Do you know *You make me feel like a Natural Woman*? The piano player began to play and Erica just shouted, "That's my song! Come on baby, dance with me." I danced with Erica and she sang along with the piano player. She whispered in my ear, "Please don't ever leave me." I saw the look in her eyes and I realized that she really did like me. At that moment, I thought to myself: I like Erica, she is a very nice lady and I want the best for her.

The rest of your life

A few weeks later I took Erica out to dinner and I said, "Do you remember when you told me that you wanted to do something with your life?" Erica replied, "Yes." I handed her an advertisement from an Airline company that was hiring flight attendants. I told Erica that she should apply. She looked at me and said, "Wow, I never thought about doing anything like that before." I said, "I think it will be good for you and you will be able to travel and see other parts of the country." Erica told me that she would look into it and about one month later Erica began training to become a flight attendant.

I was so happy for her and Erica was proud of herself. When she received her first paycheck she took me out to dinner. Erica looked at me and said, "I don't think you are really into me." I said, "Erica, I really like you. I just have a lot on my mind. I feel like I have to make a move and do something different with my life." Erica replied, "What's stopping you? I think that it will be better for the both of us if we take a break from each other and get our lives together." I gave Erica a big hug and when we finished dinner we went our separate ways. I will always remember Erica because she was such a fun person to be around. I am proud of her for taking control of her life and becoming a responsible woman. We are still good friends.

The car incident

I was leaving Walgreen's on a Friday night when a man bumped into me with his vehicle. I tapped his car with my hands to let him know that he was about to run me over. He jumped out of his vehicle and shouted, "Stop hitting my damn car." I said, "You weren't looking and you backed into me as I was walking to my car. The man swung at me and hit me right in the jaw. We began fighting in the parking lot. His female companion told him that they needed to go. He jumped into his car and drove off. I went to my Ford Explorer and followed him. I pulled up next to him and pointed my gun at him. He ran into a pole and I pulled over, placed my gun back in my off duty holster. I put on my brass knuckles and proceeded to his vehicle I reached through the window and pounded him several times across his skull. I heard sirens and the next thing I know the 21st district police officers were pulling me off of him. His female friend said, "He has a gun." The officers searched me and I told them that I worked out of Englewood and then I showed them my badge. I told them that this man hit me with his car, and then struck me in the jaw and ran off. They arrested the man and I went to the police station and signed the complaint.

Club Mayhem

I ran into one of my friends at club Mayhem one night after I left work. We began to shoot the breeze with each other, but I noticed that he appeared to be nervous, and I asked him if he was okay. He said that he was trying to talk to one of the ladies when some guy approached him and told him to get the hell away from his lady. My friend apologized to the guy saying that he did not know that. The guy told him to shut up and keep moving. My friend told him to go to hell and walked off. I told him to forget about it because it's over, but my friend said that he overheard the guy tell his friend that they should beat his ass. My friend told me that he didn't feel good about it and so he was going home.

I told him that I would leave with him and go somewhere else. As we were walking to our cars my friend looked behind him and he saw the guy who he had the altercation with along with two other men. Without looking back I took out my brass knuckles and put them on. My friend turned around again and said one of them has a baseball bat in his hand. I gave my friend my brass knuckles and pulled out my nine-millimeter berretta and as I turned around I racked the slide to send a round into the chamber and then a fired a round in the sky. Those dudes took off running so fast that I thought I was watching a track meet. My friend and I looked at each other and laughed. I told him that they didn't know who they were fucking with! My friend and I went to another club and he paid for my drinks all night!

Again, I had some crazy experiences off duty and in a very sick and twisted way I enjoyed my altercations. I wasn't looking for trouble, but I didn't back down from it either. I felt like I could go toe to toe with the craziest person on the street and I had my guns to back me up.

Chapter 6

The first district

Downtown

In 1999 I transferred to the 001st district, which primarily covers downtown Chicago and the west loop. I figured that I had been working in some of the most dangerous districts in the City of Chicago and it was time for me to take it easy. I was losing my edge on the street. I no longer got a rush out of going upside a "bad guy's" head. When I began working in the first district the station was located at 1121 south state, but about six months later a new station opened at 1718 south state. I enjoyed working in the first district, and just like the previous districts that I worked in there were many fine and dedicated police officers serving the people of Chicago.

The first district was considered to be a "slow" (low crime) district, but while I was working midnights (11:00PM-7:00AM) I found myself getting into a little action. One night I was working with a guy name Lanky. Lanky was an older gentleman, but he was a rookie. He taught in the public schools for a number of years before he joined the police department. Lanky was excited about being a police officer. He asked me many questions about my years in Englewood. I told Lanky that he is in the right place; right here in the first district where it is nice and peaceful and where the citizens are happy to see you.

Lanky said, "I want some action." I just looked at him and smiled. Lanky said, "Man I want to do some real police work." I told Lanky that this is the best kind of police work that there is; saying hello to the citizens and having them greet you with respect. Lanky told me that he wanted to transfer to one of the fast districts so that he could put in some work. I told

Lanky that it's all bullshit. I said, "Lanky, I don't mean any offense, but you are too old to be out here trying to wrestle with some of these clowns. You are cool right here in the first district. The "bad guys" in the Wood aint nothing but thugs, gangbangers, drug dealers and killers and they are all worse than Godzilla!"

All of a sudden we received a call of a stolen motor vehicle at Randolph and Michigan. Lanky got real excited. As I was driving he was itching with excitement in the passenger's seat. We observed the vehicle fitting the description. Lanky got on the radio and said, "Squad we are about to pull over the vehicle." We pulled the vehicle over and placed the men in custody. I was thinking to myself that I transferred to this district to write tickets not to chase "bad guys".

The one who got away

As I said earlier things can happen extremely fast on "the streets". One afternoon my partner and I were called into the 001st district police station to transport a prisoner to the hospital. We proceed to the station and we transported an offender to Mercy Hospital. The man had a cast that covered his entire left leg. He said that he was in a great deal of pain and needed some medication. When we arrived at the hospital we took him to the triage nurse who got him ready to see a doctor. While we were waiting my partner asked me to watch the offender so he could go and make a call. I said, "No problem." I was talking to the offender and he told me about his wife and children and he told me that he was an upstanding man. I didn't really pay too much attention to him. I had other things on my mind. His words just started to bounce off the wall.

I left him sitting down alone as I went to make a phone call. I could see him as I was talking on the phone in the other room, which was just a few feet away, but one minute I happened to look away and the next minute he was gone! "SHIT" can get not so funny real fast! When my partner returned he asked me where the offender was. I said, "I turned my back for one minute and he was gone." We frantically began to look for the offender. We searched the hospital through and through and asked the doctors if they had seen a man with a cast on his left leg and they responded no. We drove around the hospital searching for him to no avail. We got on the radio to notify the dispatcher so that other officers could join in the search.

Needless to say, we didn't find the offender that night, and the ride back to the police station was one of the longest of my life. I could already anticipate the jokes the awaited me. I say me and not us because my partner told me to watch the guy and it was my responsibility. When we arrived at the station we spoke to our beat sergeant and watch commander. This was protocol, and I didn't dread this conversation like I dreaded check off. Check off is where you turn in your numbers at the end of the tour of duty. For example, each unit would hand in a sheet with their activity.

Activity meaning how many arrests you made, how many tickets you wrote, and how many guns did you recover and so on. While you are waiting to check off, your fellow officers are all standing around shooting the breeze, and talking about their day on the street, and when they really have something to talk about: Look out!!!! The eagerly ask: What happened? How did you let a man with one leg get away from you? These are excellent questions, but it is so embarrassing when the joke is on you. The detectives found the offender the next day when they went to his house and he was eating breakfast with his wife. But for the most part, the other officers didn't talk about me that bad, but they did laugh at me for at least six months, and I deserved it.

In the line of duty

I was sleeping soundly when I received a call from Sweet O telling me that one of our friends and fellow officer had just been shot and killed during a shoot-out. The officer was working in the seventh district when he was killed in the line of duty. When I heard the news I was in shock. I could hear crying in the background from some of the officers in the seventh district. I told Sweet O that I was on my way down to the seventh district. I put my clothes on and headed downstairs. I jumped in my Ford Explorer and drove to 6120 S. Racine. When I got to the station I observed the somber mood. There was a great deal of pain and anger on the face of many of the officers. I talked to Sweet O and she just seemed as if her mind was a million miles away. After spending time with my fellow officers I headed home and took inventory of my life.

I was sitting in the car with a friend of mine after we attended the funeral of our friend and fellow officer who was killed in the line of duty. I told him that I was thinking of leaving the police department and return to school to study theology. My friend said that he did not think that it was a good idea. He said, "You are making a decent living, why would you leave? And why are you going to study theology? You will never make any money with that." I said I want to study theology because I want to engage in some form of ministry and as a man of faith I want to continue to grow in my knowledge of scripture and in my relationship with God. I also want to do something to help others. He said, "I know the death of our fellow officer has you shaken up a bit, but you have to be strong and you have to be smart."

Shortly thereafter, I attended a funeral of a friend of mine who attended the college seminary with me. His parent's house caught on fire, and he entered the house and rescued his mother from the fire, but when he went back inside to get his father, he never returned. He died from smoke inhalation, his father also died in the fire. The funeral services for my friend and his father was held at Providence Roman Catholic Church on the south side of Chicago. When I entered the Church there were pictures of him and his father around the Church. I greeted the family and then I proceeded to view the bodies. His four brothers were standing strong by their brother and fathers caskets and they greeted the people with such warmth. I noticed the rosary that my friend and his father had wrapped around their hands displaying the great faith that these men had.

The priest delivered the homily, and talked about the meaning of their lives. He mentioned the selfless act of the son in rescuing his mother. The priest's words were very comforting and it made me take inventory of my life. The priest noted that my friend and his father were both faithful members of the Church and always giving of their time and service. The funeral was powerful and in my view it was evangelization at its best. The priest encouraged the family to continue to place their faith in God. He talked about Jesus and the Resurrection, reminding the mourners that there is a time and place for everything.

The music that was played was very soothing. The choir sang one of my favorite songs, *Be not Afraid*. The funeral Mass was like a big family gathering, even though there were people that had recently came into contact with my friend due to his new job. The priest ended the funeral Mass with a powerful prayer. I felt the presence of God during the Mass. I left the Mass thinking of my friend and his father, saddened by their deaths, but inspired because I was reminded that Jesus is Lord!

Listening to the Holy Spirit

After nine years on the force I went from being a naïve kid to my own version of Monster. I evolved from being a zealous neophyte to an amoral actor. I submit that like most people in the world I was seduced. I felt like I was doing what I had to do to survive. I took all of the spiritual power that the Lord gave me and funneled it into chasing women and tricking off. On the street I saw a great deal of death, destruction, and disorder. It wasn't until my friend and fellow officer was killed that I began to listen to the Holy Spirit. I know that the Holy Spirit is always present, however; life on the mean streets made me callous and clogged my ears to the voice of the Holy Spirit. Nevertheless, the priest's message empowered me to "be not afraid." I heard God calling me, but as I thought about pursuing the priesthood, celibacy seemed ridiculous.

The road to Damascus

Initially, I only half-heartedly considered the priesthood. The In Search program of the Archdiocese of Chicago is a program for post college age men who are interested in the priesthood. I refused to join. However, I did participate in many of the activities. This was a powerful experience for me because it helped me to get back in the routine of having a strong prayer life. I was able to meditate on the scriptures and listen to other men talk about their life experiences and reflect about their call to the priesthood.

Fr. Richard Mueller, taught New Testament and Spirituality at Niles College seminary, and he is in charge of the In Search program. He is a kind man deeply rooted in the faith and he has a deep spirituality. Fr. Mueller gave the group the book, *"Poverty of Spirit,"* by Johannes B. Metz to be a guiding light for us as we went through the discernment process. This book inspired me because it allowed me to get in touch with who I am as a human being. It allowed me to get in touch with my spirit, in other words it allowed me to reflect upon the wonderful and unlimited possibilities that awaits those who rely on God's word. It helped me to focus on the things that are really important in life. The important things are everything that God has given us, free of charge. God has given us our minds, hearts, and souls so that we can do wonderful things for God and for each other.

Johannes Metz says that becoming a human being involves more than just being born. And as human beings we cannot take our being for granted because we are always challenged and questioned from the depths of our boundless spirit. There is something profound and unique to being human. I would assert that this uniqueness stems from our relationship to God and the call that God has placed in each individual's heart. As I listened to the men share their faith journey, and talk about how God has been operative in their lives my faith life was strengthened. I completed the program and left feeling good about my faith, but I was not quite ready to leave my job and go to the seminary.

I was still thinking about all of the practical things that I felt prohibited me from going to the seminary at that time. I was telling myself that I couldn't be a priest because I am not worthy. I can't be a priest because I have a strong desire to have a family. I can't be a priest because I constantly fall short of the glory of God. Shortly thereafter I fell back into my old routine. I got off work at midnight and then I would head to one of my watering holes to relax and wind down from the stress of the day.

However, the call of the Holy Spirit grew stronger. I began to question everything. The next few years of my life were spent in prayer and introspection. I constantly asked myself if this is for me. What has the Lord called me to be? While I enjoyed working as a police officer, I felt the Lord calling me, but what was that call all about? The Lord's call seems to eat at your soul and tug your heart. Nevertheless, I placed the "call" on hold and continued business as usual.

I spent time reflecting on the officers that I had known personally who were killed in the line of duty. They were good men with families and they served the citizens of Chicago with great pride. I spent time in sorrow and in prayer, and I said to myself that I have to do something different with my life. I like the job of a police officer, but the Lord has called me to do something different. The Lord has called me to proclaim the Good News. I still couldn't be a priest. I couldn't be celibate. My great compromise was to explore the Protestant traditions.

Part II

Transformation

Chapter 7

Candler School of Theology, Emory University

Candler

I was searching for a place to fulfill my dream of proclaiming the good news of Jesus Christ and I needed a place to prepare me to fulfill this mission. After careful research and much prayer I applied to Candler School of Theology at Emory University. Candler is a fine institution and they have a wonderful and talented faculty. Candler is home of the second largest theological library in the country. The very first day that I arrived at Candler for orientation, I knew that I had made the right choice.

I could feel the positive energy in the atmosphere. There was a great deal of excitement from the students there because they were exactly where the Lord had called them to be, and they were ready to prepare themselves for some form of ministry. My first week at Candler entailed orientation, making out my class schedule, and meeting new friends and classmates.

I had to fly home after a few weeks at Candler to pick up the rest of my personal belongings. When I returned on September 11th 2001 I got off the plane and walked through Hartsfield Airport. I looked up at one of the television screens and in disbelief I saw the horrible tragedy that occurred. Terrorist, using our own planes filled with people, destroyed the Twin towers of the World Trade Center. I made it back to the campus and they were prayer vigils for the many people who lost their lives in that tragedy. It seemed as if the American people as a whole began to adopt a prayerful attitude.

Immediately tension developed between Muslims and Christians. I heard many people saying that this was the beginning of a holy war. What happened on September 11, 2001 was a horrible tragedy. I heard so many things on the news that were demeaning of Muslims, and this was coming from some people of other religious traditions. People of faith must all be on guard against using violence in the name of God. And we must not stereotype a particular religion because some members of a particular faith work against the God they claim to serve. It is so important for people of faith to be able to have a fruitful and respectful dialogue regarding faith and society. Interreligious and interfaith conversations are important if we plan to make the world a better place.

During the next few weeks at Candler we had several discussions about the role that Christians play in calming the fears of people and against the mounting stereotypes against Muslims. If we have learned anything, it's that unless we submit to the spirit of God we will continue to have religious conflict locally and internationally.

I met so many wonderful people at Candler and I can honestly say that my time at Candler were three of the greatest years of my life. Candler is a United Methodist seminary, and so you might ask what is a Roman Catholic doing studying there? My answer is that I had pretty much ruled out becoming a priest because I wanted to get married and have a family. Candler is an ecumenical school of Theology. They have students from several different denominations. Yes, there are other Catholics studying there as well. Emory University also has a Catholic center.

During my first year at Candler I met some interesting people. Coming from the south side of Chicago it can be easy for one to become isolated. One of the many things that impressed me about Candler was the large enrollment of African-American men and women. I met brothers and sisters who knew their purpose in life. There were several brothers from Morehouse College, Fisk University and other historically black colleges and universities who had a great deal of swagger. Some of them were PK's (Preachers kids) who had grown up in their fathers or mothers church. There were also strong African-American sisters from Spelman University and Clark College who had the gift of proclaiming the good news. All of this was fascinating and inspiring to me. There were many outstanding young ministers at Candler, and some were also pastoring churches. I loved it when they would hear something relevant in class. They would then say, "Now *that* will preach!" The classes were inspirational and challenging.

The Faculty

Candler's faculty is top notch. Dr. Russell Richey was the dean when I was there from 2001 until 2004. The current dean is Dr. Jan Love. There is one powerful, preaching sister there by the name of Dr. Teresa Fry Brown, affectionately known as Dr. T. Dr. T is the professor of homiletics and she is a tremendous teacher and preacher. Dr. T's classes fill up super-fast, and I didn't have the pleasure of being a student of hers, but I did sit in on one of her classes and I have heard her preach on several occasions. She gave all of the students a scripture passage when we entered the classroom. She gave us a chance to look up the passage and then she would point to a student and say, "Get up and preach." Now as a "guest" I thought that I wouldn't have to do anything but observe. But Dr. T. wasn't having it. She looked at me and said, "Get up and preach!"

My palms began to sweat and my mouth was dry but I did my best to deliver an impromptu sermon. I know that it was lukewarm; the students knew that it was lukewarm; therefore you know that Dr. T knew that it was horrible. Nevertheless, she critiqued my sermon in a very gentle manner and she praised me for the things that she thought I did well.

Candler is also home to the prominent New Testament scholar, Dr. Luke Timothy Johnson and Dr. Michael Brown, a New Testament scholar, and ordained African Methodist Episcopal minister. Dr. Noel Erskine is another wonderful teacher. He is a professor of systematic theology. I signed up for his introduction to systematic theology but the class was full. I went to see him to ask if he could let me in his class. The good Doctor looked at me, and in all sincerity he said," I wish I could my brother but I am at the limit and the administration is strict on this policy."

I appreciated his straight forwardness and so I had to take introduction to systematic theology with Dr. Stefan Lösel. Little did I know, but this was the catalyst to my road to the priesthood. Dr. Lösel is a good man and an excellent theologian. He is a Lutheran minister from Germany. One of the books that we read in his class was James Cone's *God of the Oppressed*. Dr. Lösel asked the class this question: "What do you believe is the heart of the gospel; liberation or reconciliation? All of the white students replied reconciliation and all of the African-American students replied liberation. We wrestled with this for a little while and I can see why we answered the question the way we did. We all come from different backgrounds and this affects the way we view the world. Nevertheless, it took me some time for me to realize that liberation and reconciliation are not mutually exclusive.

One of the many good things about Candler is that students are encouraged to ask the difficult questions. We discussed racism, sexism, classism, materialism in the context of theology and I will argue that it made us all better because we were able to stretch our imagination and move outside of our comfort zone.

The gospel has various cutting edges to it. In my view, when we refuse to look at the gospel message from a holistic point of view we shortchange ourselves and miss out on the awesome saving power of the good news. The classes and the contextual education settings allowed for fruitful dialogue and it helped the students grow intellectually and spiritually. Contextual Education combines academic instruction with opportunities for formation in ministry and leadership in churches, social service agencies, hospitals and other clinical and social settings.

My first year contextual education site was at a woman's homeless shelter. This was a powerful experience because I was able to learn about the struggles of many of the women and yet they were strong and they were there for temporary shelter and to find employment.

The Mrs.

During my first year at Candler, I met a beautiful young lady from Chicago. She's 5 ft.3, perfect for me, nice and carefree—nice juicy lips and round voluptuous hips . . . just the way I like it! We were kindred spirits. Her thoughts were my thoughts; my laughter was her laughter; her dreams were my dreams, or so it seemed. She was a joy to be around and easy going. She didn't seem too pressured by anything. When I was with her, I was at ease.

She is intelligent and hardworking. She worked full time, and went to school full time. And hanging with me, sent her into overtime. It's a wonder she ever got any sleep. We spent time going to movies and concerts, and out to eat. I fell in love; and subsequently, I asked her to marry me. She said yes. Indeed our love was flourishing. However, during the course of our relationship I found myself hearing the call to the priesthood. I expressed this to her, but she didn't want to hear it . . . and understandably. Nevertheless, I had to be true to myself and to *the call* that was eating at my soul. It was a difficult and painful decision for me to make, but I had to break off the engagement. It caused me a great deal of pain and anguish but the Lord had other plans. She is married now and doing well.

The Holy Spirit and the Priesthood through Vatican II

One of my favorite classes was "Roman Catholic Thought" taught by Dr. Lösel. This was the first time that I had studied the Vatican Council II documents and I was blown away by the Spirit and wisdom of the Church. It is in these documents that I most clearly discerned the Holy Spirit and my call to the priesthood. Ironically, it was at a Protestant institution that I was able to truly appreciate Holy Mother Church. I embraced my Roman Catholic tradition at Candler, not out of frustration but out of an appreciation for other Christian traditions and a newfound appreciation and love of my own Roman Catholic tradition.

Vatican II is the twenty-first ecumenical council of the Catholic Church. It began under the leadership of Pope John XXIII on October 11th 1962 and closed under Pope Paul VI on December 8th 1965. There are sixteen documents that came out of Vatican II. There are four Pastoral Constitutions, The Dogmatic Constitution on Divine Revelation, *Dei Verbum*, Dogmatic Constitution on the Church, *Lumen Gentium*, Constitution on the Sacred liturgy, *Sacrosanctum Concilium*, and the Pastoral Constitution on the Church in the Modern World, *Gaudium et Spes* that are among the sixteen documents. And these four documents express a great deal of the Church's faith. When I read these documents I learned more about the Roman Catholic tradition and I was able to fully embrace the teachings of the Church.

Vatican Council II ushered in a new way in which the Church proclaimed herself to be in relationship to an ever-changing world. Vatican Council II was important for the Church because the Church presented her teachings in a clear and orderly fashion. The Roman Catholic Church had to make a statement regarding social justice, poverty, and the importance of maintaining a Catholic identity.

Chapter 8

Why I am proud to be Roman Catholic

Roman Catholic Social Justice Teachings

I am proud to be Roman Catholic because I am a man of faith who believes in Jesus Christ. Jesus Christ is our starting point and because of this the Church proclaims the value of human life and the dignity of every human being. Jesus identifies with every human being, especially those in need. Again, I respect the Protestant traditions, but I love Holy Mother Church because of her wisdom.

Gaudium et Spes is Latin and it means joy and hope. In *Gaudium et Spes* (Pastoral Constitution on the Church in the Modern World, 1965), I was struck by the awesome respect for the value of human life that the Church has and articulates through *Gaudium et Spes*. The document gives an overview of the Church's teaching about human beings and our relationship to the world with regards to economics, poverty, social justice, culture, science and technology and ecumenism.

The opening words of the document state, "The joys and hopes, the grief and anguish of the people of our time, especially those who are poor or afflicted, are the joys and hopes, the grief and anguish of the followers of Christ as well (*Gaudium et Spes*, n.1). The Church proclaims that those who identify with Jesus must also identify with the human race. As I was reading this I thought about the poverty and violence that I saw on the streets as a police officer and from reading the document it is clear that the Church has something to say about these social ills.

The Church is concerned about social justice and has a rich tradition of social justice teaching which respects the rights and dignity of all people. I love the Church because the Church is rooted and grounded in the love of Jesus Christ, and under the guidance of the Holy Spirit, the Church applies the gospel message of Jesus Christ to the world. The Church looks at the world at large and in doing so She addresses how individuals and groups should apply the gospel to the structures and institutions of the world.

The Church is relevant because She speaks to all of the issues that take place in the structures and institutions that affect the lives of human beings. The Church proclaims the truth at all times and rejects any teaching that denigrates another human being. The Church teaches that social justice rests on the profound respect for each person. The social justice teachings of the Church inspire us to put our faith into action so that we can better spread the gospel message of love, justice, and compassion to the world.

The Mystery of the Church

When I began to tell my family and friends that I was going to begin studies to become a priest some of them looked at me with the hermeneutics of suspicion. One of my Baptist friends told me that I should talk to her uncle who is a pastor because the Catholics do not believe in God and they worship idols. Another friend told me that she didn't believe in a Church that worships Mary and yet another friend didn't know that Catholics were Christian. Some people look at me, and say, "How can you as an African-American man be Catholic?" They point to the racism that exists in the Church and the racism that many African-American Catholics have endured. I have also had several protestant friends tell me that the Catholic Church is not biblical and they do not understand why I won't become a protestant minister.

My reply to them is this: The Church is beautiful. She is the first Christian Church and it surprised me to find out that some people do not know this. First of all, I would like to address the issue of racism because it is real and many of God's faithful have been harmed and scarred by this sin. One of the parishioner's at St. Ailbe informed me that when she moved into her home the neighborhood consisted of 95 percent of white people. She went to the Church and asked to speak to the pastor. The pastor took her into his office and she told him that she wanted to join the Church. She said that the pastor just looked at her and didn't say one word. She informed me that she went home and cried.

Prejudice and racism are real and I will be the first to admit it. But I agree with Father Richardt, in his response to the question of Fr. Augustus

Tolton, "Can you tell me why white people hate us?" Fr. Richardt states, "The Church always stands for right and justice. Members of the Church, however since they are human beings, often fall short of the ideals of Christ and His Church (*From slave to Priest*, P. 111). I know that racism exists. St. Augustine said that the world is marred by sin, but God can bring forth good out of evil. I have had some wonderful white teachers and priests who were dedicated to serving all of God's people.

The Church teaches that Jesus Christ instituted the sacrament of Holy Orders at the Last Supper on Holy Thursday when he also instituted the sacrament of Holy Eucharist. These sacraments are connected because without Holy Orders, there can be no Mass. The primary purpose of the priesthood is to celebrate the Mass.

It has been frustrating for me to constantly defend my faith to other Christians. Nevertheless, in doing so I continue to realize the wisdom and beauty of Holy Mother Church. In *Fire in the Bones*, Albert Raboteau states, "Catholic blacks as a religious minority, have defended their religion to the black protestant majority by asserting the universality of the Church. Black Catholics as a racial minority, have attacked discrimination and continually faced their own particularity as a people set apart. Religious universalism and racial paticularism have been the two poles of Black Catholic consciousness, rising out of their singular position as a minority within a minority." (Raboteau, 135)

As Roman Catholics we are a part of the Universal Church. We have an ancient liturgy and tradition that I am proud of. Unfortunately many people perceive the Catholic Church in the United States as a white institution. Nevertheless, the universal nature of the Church allows for diversity within the unity of the Church.

> "Though our liturgy is Catholic in that it is open to welcome the spiritual contributions of all peoples which are consistent with our biblical faith and our historical continuity, it is also Catholic in that everything that is done in our worship clearly serves (and does not interrupt) this ritual action of Word and sacrament which has its own rhythm and movement, all built on the directions, rites, and forms of the Roman Catholic liturgy as they are approved and promulgated (See J-Glenn Murray, SJ, The Liturgy of the Roman Rite and African American Worship," in LMGM.).

Black and Catholic

As African-American Catholics we trace our roots back to Simon of Cyrene the first African mentioned in the Gospel of Matthew who carried the cross of Jesus. We trace our roots back to a vibrant Church that existed in North Africa in the second and third century. We trace our roots back to St. Monica, the mother of St. Augustine who was a woman of great faith who prayed that her son would turn against evil. We trace our roots back to African saints such as Cyprian, Anthony of Egypt, Moses the black, Perpetua, Felicitas, and Thecla. We trace our roots back to the conversion of the Ethiopian Eunuch in the book of Acts. The eunuchs conversion predates the conversion of St. Paul and St. Cornelius.

In "*The History of Black Catholics*", Fr. Cyprian Davis states, "In the history of the Church, Ethiopia occupies a special place. Here we have an African Church that has its roots in the early church. Before the Church was established in Ireland or Anglo-Saxon England or in any country of northern Europe, a Catholic Church linked to St. Athanasius blossomed in an African culture. Despite any doctrinal differences that arose later, the Ethiopian Church is a reminder that Africa forms part of the rich culture of Catholicism." (Davis, 8)

Black Catholic history reaffirms an old truth: the Church must never be confused with any particular ethnic group, race, culture or time. The Church does indeed transcend race, but only by including all races within its embrace as equally valuable children, whose differences and unique contributions help to build up the body of Christ.

It would be silly of me to say that there are not people in the Church who are racist. "Continuously, black Catholics have maintained that the Church knows no race. Dan Rudd argued that blacks should convert to Catholicism because it erases the color line. The universalism of the Church was construed as conclusive evidence for the truth claims of Catholicism." (Raboteau, 135)

One True Church

Lumen Gentium submits the truth claim that the Roman Catholic Church is the one true Church instituted by Christ. It is the universal Church, which receives its unity from the Triune God. (Father, Son, Holy Spirit) The Church is a sacrament, a symbolic disclosure of God's love for humanity. Christ assumed his mission from the Father with obedience. Christ is present in the Church and continues his mission of the salvation of the world. For Roman Catholics, Sacraments are outward signs of inward grace, instituted by Christ for our sanctification. The Catechism of the Catholic Church states:

> Christ instituted the sacraments of the new law. There are seven: Baptism, Confirmation (or Chrismation), the Eucharist, Penance, the Anointing of the Sick, Holy Orders, and Matrimony. The seven sacraments touch all the stages and all the important moments of Christian life: The y give birth and increase, healing and mission to the Christian's life of faith. There is thus a certain resemblance between the stages of natural life and the stages of the spiritual life" (CCC #1210).

A sacrament is a sign that denotes communion with God.

All of humanity is called to a union with Christ, and that union is fulfilled through the Roman Catholic Church. "The mystery of the Holy Church is already brought to light in the manner of its foundation. For the Lord inaugurated his Church by preaching the good news of the coming Kingdom of God, promised over the ages in the scriptures: 'The time is fulfilled, and the Kingdom of God is at hand' (Mk 1:15; see Mt 4:17)." (Vatican Council II, LG 5) The mystery of the Church is linked to the life, death, and resurrection of Jesus and it entails Christ pouring out his spirit upon his disciples. With this, the Church received the gift necessary to sustain herself in proclaiming and establishing the Kingdom of God among all the peoples of the world.

One of the many things that I like about the Church is her structure. The Roman Catholic Church has a hierarchy and structure that enables the Church to function efficiently. The Church traces her roots back to the apostles. "This is the unique Church of Christ which in creed we profess to be one, holy, catholic, and apostolic which our Saviour, after his resurrection, entrusted to Peter's pastoral care (Jn 21:17), commissioning him and other apostles to extend and rule it, and which he raised up for all ages as the pillar and mainstay of the truth." (Vatican Council II, LG 9) The Roman Catholic Church receives its structure from Christ who instituted the Church, and its wisdom rests in the authority of the Church.

There are other Christian denominations that are in existence and the church respects the gifts that they share with God's people. However, The Roman Catholic Church argues that they contain partial truth; they are not the Church that Christ the Lord founded. The Roman Catholic Church is concerned about these divisions among the churches that believe in the Triune God, (Father, Son, Holy Spirit) and there is a desire that these departed sisters and brothers return to Holy Mother Church. "Certainly, such division openly contradicts the will of Christ, scandalizes the world, and damages the sacred cause of preaching the gospel to every creature." Christ is not divided and, therefore, the Church should not be divided. I agree with this statement because we have so many different Christian denominations divided along doctrinal lines.

The second Vatican Council celebrates the proclamation of the gospel and the adherence to Christ and the baptism of other communities while still lamenting the divisions between Christians.

There are some specific challenges to Holy Mother Church in that each particular denomination claims to know the truth and many of them claim that their authority is the Bible. I have had Jehovah's Witnesses come to me and ask me to join their congregation. When I tell them that I am Roman Catholic they look at me with confusion and sadness. They tell me that I am wasting my time with the Catholic Church.

I don't get upset because I know that the Church is rooted in the Truth of Jesus Christ. The Church is rooted in Scripture. The scripture says, "Always be prepared to make a defense to anyone who calls you to account for the hope that is in you, yet do it with gentleness and respect." (1Pet. 3:15) I have asked those Jehovah's Witnesses who have approached me to respect my belief and I've told them time and time again that I love my Church.

The Roman Catholic Church views herself as a holy institution that received its mission from Christ to spread the gospel. It charges that other churches that have departed from her with the sin of separation and admits her part in the sin of division. The division can be a sense of confusion and so it is imperative that we respect each other as we strive for unity and the Church is open to dialogue. Pope John Paul II did not like the division between Catholic and Orthodox and Catholic and Protestant. My experience at Candler enlightened me and made me aware of the need to pray for unity and the grace of reconciliation.

As Christians we must be resolute in bringing about Christian unity. Satan, the enemy loves the division among Christians because it prevents us from working effectively together. A united Church has unlimited potential and could bring so much healing to the world. As Christians, regardless of our denomination, race, creed, or color, we must work together to transform our world. This transformation can only take place when all people are respected because of their inherent dignity as human beings. As Christians we must work towards justice, peace, an equitable distribution of the world's resources for the benefit of all of God's children.

Nothing but the Truth

The Roman Catholic Church respects the truth that is contained in other faiths and believes that it is important for people of faith to work together. We have to treat those of other denominations with respect and humility. I believe that it is necessary for all Christians to do what we can to spread the message of Christ. We do have our differences, but there is a common belief and that is the truth that Jesus is Lord.

The Church is Hierarchical

Lumen Gentium contends that there is a hierarchy of truth in the Church. Christ is the head of the Church, and as people of God, we are called to be a part of the unity of the Church. The Roman Catholic Church entails truth that was revealed through Christ, and continues to sustain the Church. "This holy synod, following in the steps of the first Vatican Council, with it teaches and declares that Jesus Christ, the eternal pastor, established the holy church by sending the apostles as he himself had been sent by the Father. He willed their successors, the bishops, should be shepherds of his Church until the end of the world."(Vatican Council II, LG18) Moreover, bishops and priests represent Christ to their people.

The Pope is the highest teaching authority in the Church and is the visible representation of Christ. The bishops are the successors of the apostles, and they take part in governing the entire Church. Jesus appointed twelve apostles to be with him and to preach the kingdom of God throughout the world. "This divine mission, which was committed by Christ to the apostles, is destined to last to the end of the world (see Mt. 28:20), since the gospel that they were obliged to hand on is the principle for all the Church's life for all time. For that very reason the apostles were careful to appoint successors in this hierarchically constituted society." (Vatican Council II, LG 20) The bishops along with the priests uphold the apostolic succession to preach the good news. It is through Christ, and the apostles as his successors that the bishops are sharers in his consecration and mission. The ministry is entrusted in various degrees through bishops, priests and deacons.

The Laity

The laity are an important part of the Church, they are the people of God to which bishops and priests are entrusted to minister. The laity plays an important role in the well being of the Church. Hans Urs von Balthasar, writing in *Razing the Bastions*, states, "The future of the Church (and today she has the greatest opportunities) depends on whether laymen can be found to live out the unbroken power of the Gospel and are willing to shape the world. (von Balthasar p.42) Our world is constantly changing, and therefore, the Church must be willing to be a mainstay in a complex world and implement those things that serve the church in an appropriate manner. The Church must be open to the world, yet hold tight to her integrity. This is a difficult balance and the Church must continue to make strides to catch up with the modern world.

The Roman Catholic Church contends that the role of the laity is obedience. The laity is secular and their vocation is to manifest Christ to others by the witness of their lives. The laity are to share the vision of the Church, and by the guidance of the clergy they are to help carry out the mission of the Church.

All members of the Church are called to a life of holiness, but there is a distinction between the clergy and the laity. This distinction does not mean that one is greater than the other; all of the faithful are equal in the sight of God. "The distinction which the Lord has made between the sacred ministers and the rest of the people of God implies union, for the pastors and the other faithful are joined together by a close relationship. The pastors of the Church, following the example of the Lord should minister to each other and to the rest of the faithful; the latter should eagerly collaborate with the pastors and teachers."(Vatican Council II, LG 32) This distinction testifies to the unity of the body of Christ. During my short time in the priesthood I have met so many wonderful and talented lay people who give of their time and talents without complaint in order to serve God and God's people.

Cardinal Francis George says, "But there are other basis for leadership among Christ's people. There is expertise, which gives a certain claim to rightful influence. There are charismatic graces, sent by the Spirit to meet the needs of a particular moment; these can be a claim to leadership if they are properly discerned. Finally, holiness of life is the first title to leadership among a people made holy by Christ's self-sacrifice." (Cardinal George, p. 186) There are so many talented and gifted people in the pews and they bring so much wisdom to the Church. I have heard it said time and time again by priests that some of the people in the pews are the holiest people you will ever meet.

The laity receives the gift of peace from Christ to be doers of the Word. It is through the spirit of Christ that the laity performs deeds that bear witness to the teachings of Christ. The laity are to be authentic witnesses of the faith as exemplified by their words and actions.

The role of the laity consists of the work of bringing others to Christ. "Christ is the great prophet who proclaimed the Kingdom of the Father both by the testimony of his life and by the power of his Word. Until the full manifestation of his glory, he fulfills his prophetic office, not only through the hierarchy who teach in his name and by his power, but also through the laity." (Vatican Council II, LG 35) The laity plays a great role in building up the body of Christ and the clergy must teach and guide the Church by proclaiming the Good News of Jesus Christ.

The Role of Mary

Mary plays a profound role for the Roman Catholic Church. There are some who believe that Roman Catholics worship Mary, but this is not the case. Mary represents obedience and love. We venerate Mary; that is we give her first honors because of her role in salvation history.

Mary was so "full of grace" and filled with the Holy Spirit in this world that she was sinless and perfectly obeyed God's command to love God with her whole mind, heart and soul. Hans Urs von Balthasar, writing in *Razing the Bastions*, contends that the Church is always present when there is a true Christian. He states, "the Church is present in her purest idea in the bodily Mother and spiritual bride of the Lord: in Mary. Thus if one speaks of an ecclesial attitude, one must mean that attitude that filled Mary, since she is the embodiment of the Church as a lived reality." (von Balthasar, p.94) Mary is an example of faith and charity, which leads to service in the world.

Mary's obedience is a model for the laity and how the laity should relate to the Church. She is a model for the priests and how the priests are to relate to their bishop. "Thus the Catholic will always remain in a childlike attitude with respect to the visible governors of the Church's ordered structure and the dispensers of the word and sacrament." (von Balthasar, p.98) Mary by her motherly love cares for the Church, and therefore, she is considered to be a helper and advocate.

Mary is the mother of God; she is blessed and revered by the Church. Mary is the mother of humankind and shows the power of Christ's mediation for us. Mary is significant in regards to the mystery of the Church because of her divine motherhood. It was due to her obedience that she gave birth to Christ by the power of the Holy Spirit.

Mary is exalted above all creatures, but the Church does not want to confuse Mary's sacred position in the Church with that of Jesus. I contend that our protestant sisters and brothers who say that we worship Mary have this misunderstanding. "Following the study of sacred scripture, the Fathers, the doctors and the liturgy of the Church, and under the church's magisterial, let them rightly illustrate the offices and privileges of the Blessed Virgin which always refers to Christ, the source of all truth, sanctity, and devotion." (Vatican Council II, LG 67) The role of Mary is significant for the Church, and Mary will always be an example for all the faithful.

Given the understanding of the role of Mary for the Church, it is now imperative that the Church defines herself for the modern world. *Gaudium et Spes* seeks to accomplish this task. As our society becomes more technologically advanced there is a tendency for people to relegate God and the Church to a secondary position in their lives. It is the responsibility of the Church to interpret the gospel in the midst of change by proclaiming the mystery of faith; Christ died, was resurrected, and Christ will come again ushering in salvation for the world.

The Church has many devotions to Mary, and one of the most popular devotion is the Rosary. The Rosary is a wonderful prayer because it allows you to pray and meditate on the mysteries from the life of Jesus and Mary. When I was studying at Mount St. Mary's I learned the Salve Regina. I really enjoyed singing the Salve Regina. It is such a wonderful prayer and when it is sung in unison it is almost as if the angels were singing themselves.

Salve Regina

Salve, Regina, mater misericordiae:
Vita, dulcedo, et spes nostra, salve.
Ad te clamamus, exsules, filii Hevae.
Ad te suspiramus, gementes et flentes

in hac lacrimarum valle.
Eia ergo, Advocata nostra,
illos tuos misericordes oculos
ad nos converte.
Et Iesum, benedictum fructum ventris tui,
nobis, post hoc exsilium ostende.
O clemens: O pia: O dulcis
Virgo Maria.

The Mission of the Roman Catholic Church

Gaudium et Spes ask the enduring question of "what does it mean to be human? This is an important question, because the way in which we view a person is linked to the way in which that person is treated. "But what is humanity? People have put forward, and continue to put forward, many views about humanity, views that are divergent and even contradictory. Sometimes they either set it up as the absolute measure of all things, or debase it to the point of despair." (Vatican Council II, GS 12) The Church must wrestle with the difficulties and speak the truth. The Roman Catholic Church makes the truth claim that there is no salvation without Jesus Christ, and that the Church plays a significant role in the salvation of the world. The Church continues to proclaim dignity and respect for all people.

Awesome Liturgy

One of the things that helped me to fully appreciate The Roman Catholic Church was Chapel service at Candler. I attended some very Spirit filled services with good music and good preaching and I thoroughly enjoyed this, but the thing that I found lacking was the liturgy of the Eucharist. It is often said, that you won't miss something until it's gone. Again, I felt a sense of satisfaction through the chapel services in the sense that the Word was being proclaimed, but I was not completely fed because I missed the structure and beauty of the Mass.

During the Roman Catholic liturgy there are signs, symbols, gestures, actions and words that bring life to the liturgical service. I missed these beautiful gems that the Church has to make the worship alive and well.

The Mass comes from the Latin term *Missa*. It was used at the end of the liturgy when the priest said, "*It miss est*" It means go the congregation is sent. I love that the Church celebrates Mass every day. As Christians we are to go out into the world and proclaim the good news in word and deed. The Mass contains two parts, the liturgy of the word and the liturgy of the Eucharist.

The Liturgy of the Word is a very important part of the Mass because the scriptures are proclaimed and a homily is given to explain the scriptures. The Catechism of the Catholic Church says that the liturgy is the 'action of the whole Christ" And those in heaven are in total union with Christ celebrate the heavenly liturgy. (CCC 1136) In the protestant tradition the emphasis is placed more on the preached word. The preached word is wonderful and powerful and the protestant preachers that I've heard at Candler do an excellent job. The Roman Catholic Church stresses the importance of the word also, but admittedly I believe that we need to do a better job of proclaiming the good news.

When we as Roman Catholics celebrate the Mass we emphasize the strength and beauty of the word and the powerful reality of the Eucharist. The *Didache* is one of the earliest Christian sources that mention the Eucharist. In *The History of the Mass*, Robert Cabie' states, "The apostles, desiring to obey the Lord's command, must have imitated Jesus' behavior at the Supper, namely by sharing a ritual meal and sharing the same words. Perhaps a witness to this is found in the *Didache*, "First for the cup…then for the bread broken…and when your hunger is satisfied…" (Cabie' 13). The word Eucharist does not just correspond to any prayer of thanksgiving but for those who are baptized Christians.

Chapter 9

Finding Your Purpose in Life

Life's Purpose

The scripture says I can do all things through Christ who strengthens me. (Philippians 4:13) I believe that all people have a purpose in this life, but we don't always find our purpose because there are many things that prohibit us from seeing the big picture. For example, some people believe that the more material possessions one has reflect how successful that person is.

I contend that the biggest obstacle in the way of the success of most human beings is fear. Fear is crippling. Fear makes us doubt that we can achieve anything good in this life. Don't get me wrong, as human beings we are reasonable people, and sometimes our fears are based on what we perceive as the challenges of everyday life. For example, one might ask how am I going to pay my bills? One might say I don't really like my job and I would do something else that I love but I won't be able to support myself or my family. I contend that many people have felt this way and these are things that one has to think about. Nevertheless, I believe that the bottom line is fear.

But I assert that fear is the work of Satan. Satan uses fear to keep us from reaching our potential in life. We can be tricked and manipulated by our fears. It may be fear of change, fear for our financial security or fear of not achieving our goals in life. We cannot let fear keep us cornered into a fixed location or keep us from moving in new directions because if we do we will be rendered helpless and this is something that Satan loves.

We see the success of others, and we have heard the stories of people fulfilling their dreams, but many of us tell ourselves that we can't do it.

This is fear and fear is the enemy of faith. I assert that we must follow our passion in life. We must do what we love. We must ask the question: Am I doing what I aspired to do? For me, the scariest thing in life was not answering my call to the priesthood. Many people judge success by the amount of one's paycheck or the square footage of one's house or the size of a person's car. I believe that success is doing what God calls you to do. St. Thomas Aquinas said that a good life is one that is oriented towards God.

We have to develop our prayer life and our relationship with God. Our minds souls and dreams are invaluable gifts but most of us don't believe how powerful these gifts are. We place value in material things that we believe will make us "somebody" and we do whatever it takes to get it. People sell drugs instead of learning to sell real estate or other goods.

The Reverend Jesse Jackson said, "If you can believe it you can achieve it." Every human being should embrace this philosophy because if we have faith in the things that we want to do, we will take the necessary steps to make to achieve our goals. This is a very powerful statement because we all have dreams but some of us fail to realize those dreams because we really don't believe that we can succeed. Far too often we prohibit ourselves from achieving because of negative thinking and a lack of faith.

Reverend Jackson also said, "My mind is a pearl I can do anything in the world." We must think positive and act like there is no way in the world that we can fail. We have to stop thinking about why we can't do something. We must develop positive images instead of the negative images that we see daily via the media. We must be willing to work hard to achieve our goals.

I would argue that Reverend Jesse Jackson's poem *I am somebody* should be taught in all literature classes because it is a classic and it speaks to all of God's children. It offers them hope and gives inspiration in a world that often tells us that we are nothing if our skin color is different or we don't have a certain amount of money, go to the "right schools" or work at a particular job.

I Am Somebody

I Am
Somebody
I May Be Poor
But I Am
Somebody
I May Be Young

But I Am
Somebody
I May Be On Welfare
But I Am
Somebody
I May Be Small
But I Am
Somebody
I May Make A Mistake
But I Am
Somebody
My Clothes Are Different
My Face Is Different
My Hair Is Different
But I Am
Somebody
I Am Black
Brown
White
I Speak A Different Language
But I Must Be Respected
Protected
Never Rejected
I Am
God's Child
I Am
Somebody

This is a powerful message that we must get across to our youth. We must let them know that they are valued not because of the things that they have but because they are children of God. We are valued as human beings because of whose we are. We belong to God. I was looking at a list of the worst paying college degrees and I thought to myself could a person be happy if they take a job just because of the salary? I would argue that you have to do what you love and then you will be successful. Making money is the result of success. "Wealth does not bring about excellence, but excellence brings about wealth and all other public and private blessings for men." (Plato Five Dialogues, p.34) If a person does what they love well the rewards will come.

Plato's theory of Forms asserts that Forms, which are ideas, are the highest form of reality. He contends that ideas are the most pure of all things. Plato argues that the Forms are the only true objects that provide us with genuine knowledge. In contrast to the Forms, Plato asserts that the material world as it seems isn't the real world. Plato calls this the shadows. Every shadow has its basis in reality and that is why we often fall victim to the shadows. The shadows are a distraction from the truth and obscure our vision. Plato describes a community whose only reality is created by the shadows of puppeteers, their puppets, and the community itself who see only the shadows on the cave wall. The people are characterized as prisoners who only engage through the false reality of the shadows created by the puppet masters, as they cannot even see each other. Reality stands apart and separate from the prisoners and is the sole domain of the puppet masters. When I read Plato's theory of the Forms I was struck by how many people still live in the shadows today.

In other words, some people believe that material goods are the key to happiness and success. The shadows can keep us from becoming who God has called us to be because living in a media driven culture can blind us to values of hard work and dedication.

John Gardner said, "An excellent plumber is infinitely more admirable than an incompetent philosopher. The society, which scorns excellence in plumbing because it is a humble activity, and tolerates mediocrity in philosophy because it is an exalted activity, will have neither good plumbing nor good philosophy. Neither it's pipes nor its theories will hold water."

St. Catherine of Sienna said, "If you are what you should be, you will set the world ablaze." This is a profound and true statement. Every human being has a purpose and call in life. When we answer that call we actualize our potential and make the world better. Furthermore, Socrates said, "The unexamined life is not worth living." (Plato's Dialogue) I assert that it is important for every individual to examine his or her life in order to ascertain if they are living out their dreams.

Some of us have self-imposed limitations. We cannot let our lives be shaped by circumstances. In examining my life I came to realize that I could answer God's call with courage. I was able to look at all of my fears and bury them in the sand and approach life with a profound spirit of joy. I was constantly telling myself that I am not worthy to proclaim the message of Christ. I can do good things for others and I don't have to become a priest. These things are true, but the ultimate truth is Jesus Christ, and in listening to my call I am aware that Jesus Christ has called me to the priesthood in spite of my weaknesses. Jesus' call transforms lives and calls us into conversion.

I could have easily spent ten more years on the police department and retired. This would have been commendable, but the Lord said that it was time to move on. My time on the Chicago Police Department was wonderful and it helped me to grow as a human being. Nevertheless, for me to remain on the job when the Lord told me to move would be an exercise in cowardice and I would just be surviving and not "living" and I would have ceased to grow. An unknown author said, "Growth means change and change involves risk, stepping from the known to the unknown." There will always be risk involved when one begins a new adventure but it is important to focus on your goal and realize the benefits involved.

Charles Taylor said, "Survivalism has taken the place of heroism as the admired quality." (*The Ethics of Authenticity*, P16. Taylor) In other words we settle to be mediocre, average, but we fear greatness. It is possible that people will say negative things about you when your life does not seem to fit the norm. Nevertheless, it is imperative that you be true to yourself. True happiness involves the full use of one's power and talents. It is important for us to become well-rounded human beings. We must develop our hearts, minds, and souls. We must realize that material goods can't define who we are as human beings. We must rely on God and realize that God makes us whole and complete. Our love we have for others and ourselves reflects a healthy sense of self.

Chapter 10

Meditating on the words of Howard Thurman

Howard Thurman

During my last year at Candler it was clear to me that I would be going to the Roman Catholic seminary to become a priest. I was developing a strong prayer life and growing in my knowledge of the Roman Catholic tradition. One of my favorite classes at Candler was on Howard Thurman. Howard Thurman was born in 1899 and he died on April 10, 1981. He was an influential American author, theologian, philosopher, educator and civil rights leader. He was Dean of Theology at Howard University and Boston University for more than two decades, wrote 20 books, and in 1944 helped found the first racially integrated, multicultural church in the United States.

Dr. Luther Smith teaches a class on Howard Thurman at Candler. Dr. Smith is a wonderful man with a deep spirit. I learned a great deal from him. Dr. Smith had the class journal their thoughts each week on a particular writing of Thurman's. The class on Howard Thurman helped me to discern my call to the priesthood because I was able to come to grips with my purpose in life and who God has called me to be. Howard Thurman says, "Don't ask yourself what the world needs, ask yourself what makes you come alive and then go do that because that's what the world needs, people who have come alive." This is such a profound statement and I found myself constantly mediating on it during my time at Candler. It also made me reflect upon my life. The reason that I went to Candler in the first place is in line with Dr. Howard Thurman's quote. What makes me come alive? Answer: Studying God's Word, Preaching the good news of Jesus Christ, working for social justice, and being in the midst of God's people. This is what brings me excitement, joy and peace.

Religious experience, actualized potential, liberation, and reconciliation are important themes for Howard Thurman and they have been very profound for me in my journey to the priesthood. As I reflected upon the writings of Howard Thurman, I was able to come to grips with my purpose in life. In the *Creative Encounter*, Thurman focuses on personal religious experience as an encounter with God. Thurman states, "In the first place the encounter with God in the religious experience gives to the individual a new focal point for his life. Ordinarily this is a matter of spiritual growth and development; for here is involved a central of the self to God: (Thurman, 65). Again, I asked myself, what is my purpose in life? Thurman provided a lens by which I could search the depths of my heart and begin my life a new by responding to God's call to the priesthood.

I knew that I had to make a change in my life. In my view, this change is called growth. Thurman contends that growth always involves the risk of failure to fulfill what is implicit in a particular life, its potential. (Disciplines of the Spirit, 46)

My three years at Candler were very rewarding. I was able to grow in my understanding of myself. And it allowed me the opportunity to get away from a place where hope had all but faded and experience life where hope is alive and well. I pray that I can bring that hope to the community in which I serve. In *Disciplines of the Spirit*, Thurman states: "There are three questions an individual must ask himself, and in his answers he will find the meaning of commitment for himself: Who am I? What do I want? How do I propose to get it? (Thurman 26) I contend that every individual has to ask this question at some point in his or her life because if you don't you could find yourself doing something to make a living that doesn't feed your soul or express who you are at your deepest core.

Thurman argues that there are so many claims and counter claims, that it is difficult to find our true selves. This is so true. We live in an age of high technology, cell phones and other material gadgets that make life so convenient for us that we often begin to rely heavily on these things, sometimes more than relying on God.

It takes courage to surrender to God and become are authentic selves, but it is necessary if we want to become whole. Thurman says that we must live our lives with a purpose. As I reflected on this statement, I was reminded of the many people that I saw on the streets of Chicago while working as a police officer. There were some people just walking the streets everyday without a purpose or a goal. There are people who have lost all hope and place their faith in drugs, alcohol, and material goods.

It is important for us to find our purpose in life because when we do so we are saying yes to God's call. This purpose stems from our encounter with God. When we encounter God we come to the realization of how uniquely gifted we are and we are able to reach down into the depths of our souls to achieve our goals and to overcome any obstacles that may be in our way.

Beyond Candler

As I began my final semester at Candler I was excited about my future. I remember driving home one day and when I turned on the radio I heard the sounds of *Higher Ground* by Stevie Wonder. I was inspired by the lyrics to the song, and as I bobbed my head to the beat, I dreamed about my future. I pictured myself as a preacher, teacher, and servant of God. As I was reflecting I realized that Candler was a part of my journey to reach my highest ground.

The song Higher Ground speaks volumes to me because it encourages people to reach their full potential in life. A few of the lyrics that rang loudly in my ear are, "I'm so glad that he let me try it again, because my last time on earth I lived a whole world of sin. I'm so glad that I know more than I did then. I'm going to keep on trying til I reach my highest ground, God is going to show you higher ground." I believe that my matriculation through Candler has been my second chance because it helped me to develop a deeper sense of purpose in life. I came to see clearly that I am on a spiritual journey and that journey began when I encountered Jesus Christ.

Our initial encounter with the Lord is the beginning of discipleship. When we encounter the Lord we are able to walk the path of righteousness. This is not to say that we won't encounter difficulties in our life, but we have the power of Jesus Christ to help us overcome.

The theme of community is a major part of Howard Thurman's thought. Dr. Luther Smith argues that reconciliation is essential in Thurman's understanding of community, and that reconciliation is linked to love. The words reconciliation and love are powerful. I often hear these words used when there is a discussion of race in America. I would assert that reconciliation is used more often. I contend that if we stress love and its relation to reconciliation, it will enable us to develop a true community and affirm and appreciate our differences.

I like Thurman's vision of community because it reflects the unity of the human family. Dr. Smith states, "This unity, as it relates to Thurman's concept of community, is characterized by its ability to allow persons to actualize their potential. In actualizing potential, persons come to recognize and realize their worth and purpose for life" (Smith, 46). This is important to me because if all human beings actualized their potential it would foster a unified community of love and peace.

One Sunday morning I attended Our Lady of Lourdes Roman Catholic Church in Atlanta, Georgia. The Mass was wonderful and uplifting. The priest spoke about Abraham's blessings. He noted that Abraham would never have received his blessings if he had remained in Haran. I thought to myself that I would never have received the blessings that I have if I had not left Chicago to attend Candler School of Theology. Abraham was making a decent living in Haran. His basic needs were met, but Haran was not all that God had in store for Abraham. Haran was a stop over, a temporary place for Abraham to live until he left Canaan. I know very well that I am not Abraham, but I compared my situation to his. When I was working as a police officer, I had job security, my basic needs were met, and I was in Chicago with my family and friends. I love my family and I enjoyed my job, but I knew that God required more from me. My job was like a stop over. It was a temporary place, but I was not meant to stay there.

When I left Chicago a new world opened up for me because people who had high hopes and aspirations constantly surrounded me. It was wonderful to see the energy and excitement of my fellow classmates. They were excited about learning. They enjoy preaching the gospel of Christ and they have a desire to serve humanity. This type of energy is contagious, and I would argue that I came to Candler with energy and hope and studying, praying, and learning at Candler made me stronger and wiser.

Chapter 11

Seminary life

A step towards the priesthood

I was reading Immanuel Kant's, *An answer to the Question: What is Enlightenment.* Whereas Kant criticized external ritual and hierarchical church order, and was not necessarily fond of religion. I found value in this essay because it is uplifting when it is placed in a proper context. In my view, Kant is calling for individuals to assert themselves and to move beyond a mere petty existence. Life is more than just eating and drinking for one's physical survival. Life is about finding and fulfilling one's potential in life.

Kant argues that it is important to leave minority and become a mature person. Kant contends that laziness and cowardice keep the great part of human beings from achieving this task. He states, "It is comfortable to be a minor! If I have a book that understands for me, a spiritual advisor who has a conscience for me, a doctor who decides upon a regimen for me, and so forth, I need not trouble myself at all" (The Cambridge Edition of the Works of Immanuel Kant, P.17). As I read this I reflected on my decision to leave the Chicago Police Department to attend Candler. I was living a relatively comfortable life, but I was called to do something else.

I assert that if I had stayed at my job that it would have hindered my growth as a human being. Kant states, "Thus it is difficult for any single individual to extricate himself from the minority that has become almost nature to him. He has even grown fond of it and is really unable for the time being to make use of his own understanding, because he was never allowed to make the attempt." (Kant, 17) There were a myriad of good reasons that I could have used to stay at my job, but like Kant, these reasons are the "ball and chain of an everlasting minority." (Kant, 17) I stepped out on faith and this is the only way that I know how to live.

My time at Candler allowed me to accept the call to the priesthood. I was living in Atlanta and so I applied to study for the diocese of Atlanta. The application process was extensive, somewhat like the police department's process. I told the vocation director that I would be graduating in the spring of 2004 from Emory University with a Masters of Divinity. I asked him how long of a process would it be for me since I already have a Masters of Divinity degree. He told me that he would look into it and get back to me. One week later, he told me that I would have to be in formation for five years. I didn't think about the length of time at that moment because my focus was on the priesthood.

I told my family that I was going to Maryland to study for the priesthood. I didn't tell them how long it would take me because I didn't want them to look at me like I was crazy. Nevertheless, they would soon find out that it would be a long and arduous road. I am so grateful that my family stood by me and supported me on my journey and I know that they often wondered if I had lost my mind. On the journey I experienced my share of trials and tribulations, but that is nothing compared to those brave men and women who have died for the faith. And as the Tertulian said, the blood of the martyrs is the seed of the Church.

I was working out at a health club in Chicago with a friend of mine, the summer before I would begin my first year of seminary. As we were walking through the gym we came across a friend of his and he introduced us. The conversation shifted to, "What do you do"? I said that I was about to begin studies for the priesthood. He asked me, "How long was the process?" I replied, "five years". He stared at me for what seems like forever, and then he said, "My cousin is a Baptist minister. He has his own church and he has been preaching since he was five years old." I did not even know what to say to this man at that time because he just seemed to be baffled at the thought of someone studying to be a minister. I guess he feels that when you hear the Lord's call you start preaching right away, just like his cousin did. I didn't feel like explaining the concept of seminary. I just wanted to get in some exercise. I knew that I had to answer my calling in my own time and in my own way.

Candidates for the priesthood are required to possess a bachelor's degree. It takes five to six years to study for the priesthood and a seminarian has to complete at least 30 credit hours in philosophy. The objective of the program of priestly formation is to help men prepare to become parish priests. The seminary helps men to grow in prayer through daily Eucharist, praying the liturgy of the hours, which is the official prayer of every priest. Men studying for the priesthood also receive spiritual direction so that they may grow in their spiritual life.

In pre-theology, seminarians are introduced to the seminary and its expectations. The academic curriculum for that year consists for the most part of the study of philosophy. In first theology, seminarians learn the methods of prayer and human formation is the primary focus. In second theology, the focus is on lived discipleship. In third theology, seminarians focus on faith sharing, and in the final year, fourth theology, the program focuses on priestly ministry and public leadership in the Church.

Two weeks before I headed out to Maryland I saw a friend from Loyola University. She asked me how I was doing. I told her that I was doing well. I said, "How are things going for you?" She replied, "Everything is going well for me also." She said, "Are you still with the police department?" I told her that I had left the police department about three years ago and that I was leaving in a few weeks to begin studying for the priesthood. She gave me the typical long stare that I usually receive when I told my friends that I was going to become a priest. She said, "I have a friend who is a minister, and you need to talk to him, I don't know about those Catholics. I know you like women. Haven't you been reading the news about all those priest molesting little boys?" I must admit I was extremely embarrassed. I am angry at the priests who have abused children. I replied, "I have seen such stories on the news and it is horrible, but it does not reflect the majority of priests who serve the Church well." She looked at me in disbelief and I just asked her to pray for me.

Seminary

I was accepted and began my studies at Mount St. Mary's seminary in Emmitsburg, Maryland. It was August 15th, 2004 and I went to O'Hare airport and boarded the plane and flew into Baltimore/Washington International Airport (BWI). Tim Gallagher, a first year theologian studying for the diocese of Atlanta picked me up and from BWI and we took the 90 minute ride to Emmitsburg, Maryland. When I arrived on the campus I found it to be warm and peaceful. I was greeted by the orientation committee and then given my orientation packet and room key. I went up to my room and unpacked my bags and began my first day as a seminarian.

The orientation was a two-week process. We were instructed in the prayer life and rhythm of the seminary. We had several speakers who spoke on various subjects. One of the workshops that I found particularly interesting and powerful was project Rachel. We had people speak to us from their experience of having had an abortion. Each speaker talked about the loss that they had felt after having had an abortion. The Church speaks of the dignity of the human being and rightfully proclaims the sacredness of life. The Church is right in its stance on pro-life from the cradle to the grave.

I met some very good men at Mount St. Mary's, affectionately known as "The Mount" although I was the only African-American student; the Mount is a culturally diverse seminary that includes students from Africa, Asia, Latin America, and the United States. Mount St. Mary's is a wonderful place to study. I couldn't really see it at the time because I was so ready to get out into the parish and do some work. I was tired of school, and all of the theory that I was hearing because I had already received a Masters of Divinity from Candler School of Theology at Emory University, and so it was difficult for me to focus.

I have never had the terms liberal and conservative used so much as I did while I was a student at the Mount. These terms made me feel uneasy. I did not like them because they seemed to divide and undermine the mission of the Church. Cardinal George says, "But a church of such factions not only cannot evangelize; it cannot think. That is the greatest practical difficulty; it seems to me, in the use of the terms "liberal" and "conservative." (Cardinal George, 170) I assert that the teachings of the Church are true and if we abide by them we can do away with these terms because we are one in the Spirit, we are one in the Lord. (Ephesians 4:2-6)

Even though I possessed a Masters of Divinity degree, Mount St. Mary's started me out in pre-theology and that meant that I had to take one year of philosophical studies on the college side. I was pissed!!!! And so, at thirty-eight years of age I was taking classes with 18-year-old college students. My first year of seminary took some getting used to. I had been living on my own since I was twenty-four years old, but now I found myself in a single room and having to share a common bathroom with the other seminarians on my floor.

The days were long. We began each day at 7:00AM with morning prayer and Mass. Classes began around 8:30 AM and then after classes we had time for studying and exercise. At 5:00 PM we had evening prayer, followed by dinner. And there was always some type of formation program during the evening. This could be a lecture on scripture, the methods of prayer or spiritual direction or a host of other theological and spiritual topics. The talks were always informative and geared to prepare us for ministry.

I had a wonderful spiritual director in Fr. Dietrich. I told him that I was struggling with the rigid nature of formation, mainly because of my age and a willingness to gain back my independence. He reminded me that many of the apostles were "second career" men when Jesus called them. Fr. Dietrich helped me to grow in my prayer life and he told me to pray for patience. Spiritual direction saved my vocation even though I would continue to struggle.

I played intramural sports with my fellow seminarians against the students in the college. It was a good time for recreation and also helped to foster camaraderie among the seminarians. Catholic seminary formation was a big adjustment for me, but I eventually made the adjustments necessary to make it through.

I was tired and worn out after my first year in the seminary. I was supposed to spend the summer working in a parish in Atlanta, but I told the vocation director that I needed some time off. He allowed me to work during the summer. I spent the time working with James Young, a good friend and the owner of Accuracy Glass in Atlanta, Georgia. The time off was good because I was able to take a step back from the structured environment of the seminary and listen to my call. I had to constantly ask myself: "What is my purpose in life?" I felt strongly about my call to the priesthood, but I didn't have the virtue of patience. I wanted to be ordained right away because I had already received my Masters of Divinity degree and had a great deal of life experience. Nevertheless, there was and still is much for me to learn.

Fr. Tolton

I returned for first theology and the first semester seemed to go fairly well. I was adjusting to seminary life and learning a great deal. As part of my formation, I worked at St. Teresa of Avila on the weekends doing tutoring and assisting as a lector and acolyte during Mass. The pastor of St. Teresa of Avila is Monsignor Raymond East. He is a gifted priest who is good at teaching, preaching, and serving the people of the parish well.

But then February came and it was like I ran into a brick wall. I caught a ride to Washington DC on a Friday and did not return until Wednesday. I slept in the train station during the night and spent my days at Howard University and Starbucks so that I could collect my thoughts. I opened up Fr. Augustus Tolton's book, *"From Slave to Priest* and I began to read it. I said to myself if Fr. Augustus Tolton endured what he did, I should be ashamed of myself for complaining. The first three black priests in the United States were three brothers, all of whom were born slaves to Michael Morris Healey, an Irishman and his slave Mary Eliza. Nevertheless, the Healey brothers did not identify themselves with the African American population. Fr. Augustus Tolton is recognized as the first African American priest in the United Sates. He was ordained in Rome on April 24th, 1886 in Rome because he was not allowed to study at an American seminary because of his race.

Fr. Tolton was constantly denied the chance to study for the priesthood in America, but he did not give up. This is an excellent example of perseverance. Too many people give up at the first hint of resistance. Fr. Tolton didn't take no for an answer. His faith in God enabled him to achieve.

The scripture says, "You may for a time have to suffer the distress of many trials; but this is so that your faith, which is more precious than the passing splendor of fire-tried gold, may by its genuineness lead to praise, glory and honor when Jesus Christ appears." (1Peter 1:6-7) When I was going through the Roman Catholic seminary formation I couldn't appreciate the total aspects of the program. I was locked in to my disdain for being in school for such a long time. Nevertheless, the scripture has a way of unlocking the horizons of our mind. For example, this passage from the book of Job speaks volumes to me because it helped me to shift my focus from myself and to put it where it belongs, and that is in the hands of God:

Job 38:1-7, (34-41)

38:1   Then the LORD answered Job out of the whirlwind:

38:2   "Who is this that darkens counsel by words without knowledge?

38:3   Gird up your loins like a man, I will question you, and you shall declare to me.

38:4   "Where were you when I laid the foundation of the earth? Tell me, if you have understanding.

38:5   Who determined its measurements--surely you know! Or who stretched the line upon it?

38:6   On what were its bases sunk, or who laid its cornerstone

38:7   when the morning stars sang together and all the heavenly beings shouted for joy?

38:34   "Can you lift up your voice to the clouds, so that a flood of waters may cover you?

38:35   Can you send forth lightnings, so that they may go and say to you, 'Here we are'?

38:36   Who has put wisdom in the inward parts, or given understanding to the mind?

38:37   Who has the wisdom to number the clouds? Or who can tilt the waterskins of the heavens,

38:38   when the dust runs into a mass and the clods cling together?

38:39   "Can you hunt the prey for the lion, or satisfy the appetite of the young lions,

38:40   when they crouch in their dens, or lie in wait in their covert?

38:41   Who provides for the raven its prey, when its young ones cry to God, and wander about for lack of food?

Job's so-called friends thought they knew all of the answers when they debated with Job. Nevertheless, rather than offering a compelling explanation of why these things happened to Job, God tells Job who God is and calls Job to worship. For those of us who want explanations for pain and suffering this is a frustrating move. No answers are given as to why these things happen. I thought to myself that I do not have any reason to complain. I thought about my call to the priesthood in the broader scheme of things. People are suffering and catching hell all around the world, and I am complaining about seminary formation.

One of my fraternity brothers picked me up and took me back to the seminary. I went back with renewed energy. After evening prayer I went to my room and before I could open the door the phone was already ringing. It was the rector of the seminary. He told me to meet him in his office. When I arrived at his office I could tell that he was upset with me. He said, "Where have you been?" I told him that I needed to get away because I was just feeling tired and burned out. He couldn't understand my frustration. He said, "You only have four years to go." I replied, "I am thirty-nine years old and I have been in school for the past five years and I have four more to go. I needed to get away and re-evaluate my call."

Back to the Chi

I told the rector that I understood his position and that I was ready to focus and finish the school year on a good note. When the school year ended, I spoke with the vocation director and told him that I still felt good about my call to the priesthood but I wanted to go back home to study for the priesthood in my hometown, Chicago, Illinois. I spoke to the vocation director Joe Noonan about studying for the priesthood in Chicago. I filled out an application and sent in the required documents. I completed my physical examination and then I went to the board for my interviews. I was accepted and began second theology at University of St. Mary of the Lake, Mundelein Seminary in the fall of 2007.

The IBCS

I was blessed to spend the summer studying at The Institute for Black Catholic Studies. The Institute for Black Catholic Studies was founded in 1980 and it is located at Xavier University of Louisiana and it prepares laymen and women as well as vowed religious, priests and deacons for a more powerful and meaningful ministry within the African-American community. Dr. Norman C. Francis is the president of Xavier University of Louisiana and Sr. Jamie T. Phelps, O.P., Ph.D is the director.

During the summer of 2007, the Institute was held at the University of Notre Dame because of hurricane Katrina. Therfore, I was able to meet other Catholics from across the country. We prayed, studied, and celebrated together. It was a moving experience and I look forward to spending another summer at the IBCS in the future. When the summer ended I began studies at University of St. Mary of the Lake, Mundelein Seminary.

Mundelein

My experience at Mundelein Seminary was wonderful. Mundelein seminary is located north of Chicago. It is the largest Roman Catholic seminary in the United States. The campus is beautiful and serene. As part of the formation program for the Archdiocese of Chicago, seminarians are required to spend a quarter in a parish. This takes place in the third quarter of second theology. I had already completed pre-theology and first theology at Mount St. Mary's and so I began my studies at University of St. Mary of the Lake (USML) in second theology. I spent the first and second quarters in formation at USML and then I spent the third quarter at St. Philip Neri on the south side of Chicago. This was a wonderful experience for me because I was working in the parish and I was finally away from school for the first time since 2001. I was able to meet many wonderful parishioners who helped me to grow in faith.

I would like to share one of my reflections that I delivered while an intern at St. Philip Neri. This sermon is printed in the spring 2008 edition of the African American Pulpit: **SERMON**

Faith is the realization of what is hope for and evidence of things not seen. Hebrews 11:1) Faith is rooted in our very being. It is a mutual possession. We could not possess the Truth if the Truth had not first possessed us. In the Gospel of John, the most important requirement for discipleship is the belief in Jesus. Last week we celebrated Easter, which reflects the central saving event of the history of salvation. Yes! It is Resurrection time. Today as we celebrate the second Sunday of Easter, we are commissioned by Christ to spread the Good News in Word and deed. And whenever we participate in the Eucharist, we are reminded of the Paschal Mystery-that is the life, death, and resurrection of our Lord.

Today's gospel tells us that the disciples were meeting in a locked room in fear of the Jews. More than likely they were meeting in the upper room where the last supper had been held. The disciples were fearful because Jesus had just been put to death; and as followers of Jesus, they felt that they would be next. But as they sat there filled with anxiety, Jesus came and stood in their midst and proclaimed, "Peace be with you." (John 20:19).

Now this gift of peace that Jesus gives to the disciples designates harmony and order. It signifies completeness and perfection. Jesus' words affect peace. It lets the disciples know that they can face the Jewish authorities with the peace of Christ. Jesus says, "As the Father has sent me, so I send you." (John 20:21). Jesus commissions the disciples to proclaim the word that God's saving plan is accomplished. *"Faith is the realization of what is hoped for and evidence of things not seen."*

Jesus then breathes on them and gives them the gift of the Holy Spirit. Now this spirit has been operative since the beginning of time. In the Old Testament, the Hebrew word for spirit is *ruhah*. This Spirit is the principle of life and vital activity. It is the same Spirit revealed in Genesis by which man became a living being. We witness aspects of the power of this spirit in the Book of Exodus as the saving force by which Israel is liberated from the Egyptians. We see the power of the Spirit in the book of Numbers when the Spirit descends upon the seventy elders to inspire prophecy. We see it in Ezekiel as he prophesied over the dry bones, proclaiming thus says the Lord God to these bones: See! I will put my spirit in you, that you may come to life" (Ezekiel 37:5) The Spirit is at work in all the prophets as a dynamic power by which God accomplishes his works.

In the New Testament, the Greek word for "spirit" is *pnuema*. And this Spirit reveals itself in a similar fashion. The Spirit leads Jesus into the desert as he begins his ministry, and it is the power by which Jesus resists Satan's temptations. In the book of Revelation, it is the spirit that allows John to give testimony to Jesus. John says, "I was caught up in the Spirit on the Lords day." (Revelation 1:10) God gives this Spirit in an answer to prayer, and this Spirit is conferred to all believers at baptism. This Spirit is in you and me. The Holy Spirit gives you the power to transcend a difficult situation. It inspires you to reach your full potential. It elevates your level of consciousness. It enables you to pray. It infuses the virtues of prudence, justice, fortitude, and temperance. It innovates, cultivates, and motivates. It empowers you to press on when there seems to be no way out, having faith that God will make a way out of no way. *"Faith is the realization of what is hoped for and the evidence of things not seen."*

The disciples receive this Holy Spirit and Jesus tells them, "Whose sins you forgive are forgiven them and whose sins you retain are retained." (John 20:23) Forgiveness means the cancellation of ones debt to God. It means to release or liberate. To forgive someone is to release them from the domination of their past history. Forgiveness can be difficult, but the forgiveness of sins has to be understood as the Spirit-empowered mission of continuing Jesus' work in the world.

Jesus' breathing the Holy Spirit on the disciples can be viewed as a new creation because those who believe in Jesus receive new life as children of God. *"Faith is the realization of what is hoped for and the evidence of things not seen."*

Now Thomas was not with the other disciples when Jesus appeared to them. The Scripture says that the other disciples said to him that they had seen the risen Lord. But Thomas did not believe. He said, "Unless I see the mark of the nails in his hands, and put my finger in the nail marks and put my hand into his side, I will not believe." (John 20:25) Now we really can't be mad at Thomas. It was Thomas who encouraged the other disciple to accompany Jesus into Judea and die with him. You see, it was only when Jesus appeared to the other disciples that they came to believe and rejoice.

The Scripture says that a week later the disciples were inside and Thomas was with them. Again, Jesus comes through the locked doors and appears in their midst greeting them again with, "Peace be with you." (John 20:26) Peace is the state of spiritual mindedness. Jesus tells Thomas that he can put his finger into his side, but Thomas does not. Instead he says, "My Lord and my God." (John 20:28) It is not touching Jesus that leads Thomas to this confession of faith, but Jesus' generous offering of himself. Jesus says, "Have you come to believe because you have seen me? Blessed are those who have not seen and have believed." (John 20:29) *"Faith is the realization that is hoped for and evidence of things not seen."*

Now it can be argued that Thomas should have believed because of the report given to him by his fellow disciples instead of demanding a sign. Nevertheless, faith is often supported by miracles, and miracles do inspire faith. But I stopped by here to tell you that a faith that relies only on miracles is inadequate and empty. "It is inferior to a faith that relies solely on the word of God. You see, seeing can be an occasion for believing, but the faith of Thomas who believes because of what he has seen is less perfect than those who believe without seeing. Faith outstrips physical seeing and brings about a spiritual vision."(Dulles, P.94) You see, without faith it is impossible to please God. (Hebrews 11:16) And that is why we walk by faith and not by sight (2 Corinthians 5:7) "*Faith is the realization of what is hoped for and the evidence of things not seen.*"

What is our mission today? I submit to you that in order for us to understand our mission that we have to read the signs of the times. Our world is in shambles. There are forces of evil at work in the world. We have to put our faith into action. We have to raise a voice of peace against the war in Iraq. We have to loosen our tongues to speak out against materialism, racism, and sexism. We have to raise a voice of peace against violence in our communities. We have to loosen our tongues to speak out against economic injustice. We have to resist a watered down prosperity gospel that lifts up material gain as the only sign of God's favor, but has nothing to say about the reality of suffering, poverty, and death in our world.

You see, suffering is a part of the human condition and it has to be grappled with. We have to avoid a superficial religion that seeks to avoid this entire dimension of the human experience. You know there are some folks who view God as just a spiritual ATM machine. There are some who view God as a magic genie in a bottle. If God does not provide for their wants and demands, then this is not their God. They espouse a weak doctrine to a people who are spiritual by our birthright. We trusted in the Lord during slavery and survived. We leaned on the Lord during segregation and survived. You see we are a people who have looked back and thanked God and have a vision for the future, knowing all along that we have come this far by faith! "*Faith is the realization of what is hoped for and evidence of things not seen.*"

I worked as a Chicago Police officer for ten years in a few of the most violent areas in the City of Chicago. I witnessed the violence of black on black crime and the injustices of a criminal justice system that is partial to locking up poor minorities. I was also disturbed by the idolatry that exists in our communities because we are a faithful people. But it seems that some of us have chosen to worship the false gods of materialism and immediate gratification. Some of our sisters dress in a manner that says that they don't know that they aren't a piece of meat. And some of our brothers carry themselves as if they have given up on life. What kind of man walks out of the house with his pants hanging off of him! Brothers, stand up and be counted! Where is your dignity and self-respect? There has to be some substance to our being. Place your faith in Jesus Christ and not in the accumulation of things that can easily be taken away. We must remember the faith of our mothers and fathers.

"Our faith in Jesus compels us to combat the politics of domination and oppression with the practice of justice and compassion." [19] Jesus is telling us what he told John. "Do not be afraid. I am the first and the last, the one who lives. Once I was dead, but I am alive forever and ever. I hold the keys to death and the netherworld." (Revelation 1:17-18). It's Resurrection time! *"Faith is the realization of what is hope for and evidence of things not seen."* **End of Sermon**

Holy Land

My experience at University of St. Mary of the Lake was fulfilling. During my second quarter of third theology, I went to study in Israel with most of my classmates. The pilgrimage was a powerful experience on many levels. Firstly, it came at an important time. I was feeling a bit tired from the day-to-day life of a seminarian. The pilgrimage enabled us to get away from the typical classroom and formation setting and it reenergized me. The pilgrimage was so gratifying because we were walking in the footsteps of our Lord. It was nice to be able to experience a different culture and pray and worship at the various biblical sites.

This experience made me feel at one with the Gospel. Being in the Holy Land really made the Scriptures come alive. We arrived in Zurich, Switzerland on 29NOV07 and spent the night there and the next day we caught a flight to Israel. We stayed in Bethlehem for the first month of the pilgrimage with the Betharram sisters and then we stayed in Jerusalem at the Notre Dame center for the second month of the pilgrimage. The first day I toured the Church of the Nativity with my friend and classmate Augustine. We walked through the city of Bethlehem observing the various sites. Bethlehem is about eight hours ahead of Chicago and it took a day or two for my body to get adjusted to the time difference. I was sleeping in three-hour shifts, and every day I would awake to the Muslim call to prayer at 5:00AM.

Sr. Kathleen Mulchay taught us a class on the spirituality of the pilgrimage. We discussed Egeria and her travels to the Holy Land. Egeria was a woman who made a pilgrimage to the Holy Land around the years 381-384. She wrote an account of her journey in a long letter to a circle of women at home. Her story is powerful because it reveals her deep faith and Egeria's writings about the Holy Land reveal the beauty of "Holy Mother Church" and gives us a view of fourth century worship in Palestine.

We visited Mar Saba, a monastery in the Judean desert. It is an amazing site. We saw the Old caves that the monks lived in during the fourth century. During one of our prayer services we prayed the Rosary together. The Rosary is divided into five decades. Each decade represents a mystery or event in the life of Jesus. There are four sets of "Mysteries of the Rosary." *(Joyful, Luminous, Sorrowful, and Glorious)* These four "Mysteries of the Rosary" therefore contain, a total of twenty mysteries. The Joyful, Luminous, Sorrowful, and Glorious Mysteries are then said on specific days of the week. During private recitation of the Rosary, each decade requires devout meditation on a specific mystery. Public recitation of the Rosary *(two or more people)* requires a leader to announce each of the mysteries before the decade, and start each prayer.

The Rosary was recited in five different languages by my fellow seminarians, each announcing a mystery in their native language. Tien announced the first joyful mystery (The annunciation of Gabriel to Mary) in Vietnamese. Augustine announced the second joyful mystery (The visitation of Mary to Elizabeth) in Swahili. Andres announced the third joyful mystery (The birth of Jesus) in Polish. David announced the fourth joyful mystery (The presentation of Jesus in the Temple) in Spanish. Leopola announced the fifth joyful mystery (Finding Jesus in the Temple) in Filipino. We had a rich and powerful experience of praying the rosary in this manner. The seminary is truly blessed because of the international flavor that it has.

The next day we celebrated Mass at St. Catherine's, the parish located next to the Church of the Nativity. The Mass was celebrated in the Arabic language. After the Mass we met with the Franciscan pastor. He welcomed us and told us about his take on the Israeli/Palestinian conflict. We shared a little of our stories with him and then we had lunch.

We visited Hebron on 10DEC07. The most famous site in Hebron is the Cave of the Patriarchs. Jews, Christians, and Muslims venerate this site. We saw the tombs of Abraham, Sarah, Isaac, and Jacob.

A few days later we visited Masada. This is the place where reportedly the Jews committed mass suicide rather than becoming slaves to the Romans. It is a very interesting place. We took a cable car to reach the highest point of the mountain. I was a little hesitant because I don't like heights, but it was a powerful experience and the sites were fabulous! We toured Qumran, where the Dead Sea scrolls were found and we went to the Dead Sea. Many of my classmates went for a float in the Dead Sea and they really enjoyed themselves. We spent the next few days at Bethlehem in study and prayer. We also had a few presentations on Islam that were very informative. I was able to develop an appreciation of the Islamic faith as opposed to the stereotypical belief that all Muslims are terrorist.

16DEC07 - We hit the road again at 7:30 AM to travel to Nazareth. It was a wonderful trip. We visited the Church of the Annunciation and celebrated Mass in the Chapel. The church has images displayed around the church of Mary and Jesus that come from all over the world.

The next day we visited Mount Tabor, which is a beautiful and breathtaking site. We had Mass at the church there and afterwards we had a nice lunch. Afterwards, I walked down the mountain with several of my classmates. It was a peaceful experience. We did not say much to each other on the walk down because we were all captivated by the beautiful scenery.

We visited the only Christian church in Naim, the site where Jesus brought the widow's son back to life. We visited Cana, the place of one of my favorite miracles-Jesus changing the water to wine. As I strolled along the roads of Cana with my friend and classmate Augustine, we came across a wine shop and we went in and purchased a bottle of red wine just because we were in Cana. Needless to say the wine was delicious! No wonder this was the first miracle that Jesus performed.

18DEC07 - We visited the Jordan valley, Jericho, and the Mount of Temptation. The mountain is huge and high. We ascended the mountain via cable car. It was very scenic. The monks there live in the mountain, in carved out cells. They have a wonderful view, but I would be scared to death to live up there. The view is nice, but if you slip off of that mountain you can cancel Christmas.

22DEC07 - We had a Christmas party for the children at the Crèche orphanage. The children had a wonderful time and so did we. My fellow seminarians, Leo and Ben, performed a hilarious donkey routine for the children. They laughed so hard and I found myself laughing even harder. The next day we celebrated Mass at a Melkite Catholic Church. The pastor, Fr. Yacoub Abu Scada was nice and hospitable. On Christmas Eve I woke up around 6am and I walked around Bethlehem for about an hour. I came back and took a nice hot shower and then went to Morning Prayer. We celebrated midnight Mass at Bethlehem University. The provost of Mundelein seminary, Fr. Baima gave an excellent homily on the true meaning of Christmas. We had a prayerful and powerful liturgy. After Mass there was a nice reception and the food and wine was overflowing. When we arrived back to Betharram I went straight to bed and slept like a baby.

Christmas was wonderful. I woke up and jumped in the shower and started singing "This Christmas" by Donny Hathaway. This was the first Christmas that I had ever spent away from home and this tune just brings back great memories of family, friends and good times. We had lunch at La Terrace restaurant. We ate and drank like kings. I walked back from the restaurant with my fellow seminarians George and Augustine. We had evening prayer and then we had a Christmas party of our own.

28DEC07 - I went down to the Crèche orphanage with a few other seminarians. One of the nuns, Sr. Sophie took us to a remote place in the desert to distribute food and water to families that live out there. The families basically live in the desert in caves. They live a very simple life and they seem to be at peace. One of the children asked one of the seminarians what it was that he was holding. He told her that it was a camera. He took a picture of her and showed it to her. When she saw a picture of herself on the digital camera she became very excited. Sr. Sophie is very dedicated and hard working. She makes sure that she can help the families out with food and clothing. The families that live in the desert say that they are happy with their way of life.

We brought the New Year end by traveling to Haifa. Haifa is the largest city in Northern Israel and it is built on the slopes of Mount Carmel. We celebrated Mass at the Carmelite chapel and stayed the night at the Carmelite monastery before returning to Bethlehem the next day.

02JAN08 - We toured Sepphoris and saw the remains of a third century city. We also visited Bet Shearim and met with the Melkite bishop Chacour. He told us about his book, *Blood Brothers*, which talks about his experience of growing up in Palestine. The next day we headed to Galilee and stayed the night at Pilgerhaus, a resort along the Sea of Galilee. We visited a nice church in Capernaum that was built on the site of the Apostle Peter's house. You can see the remains of a fifth century church below. We visited Magdala, the place where Mary Magdala is from and then we went for a boat ride on the Sea of Galilee. I immediately thought about our Lord telling the disciples to cast their nets to the other side so that they could catch some fish.

05JAN08 We celebrated Mass at the Primacy of Peter, which sits along the Sea of Galilee. We visited Tel Dan, where King Jereboam ruled. We left Pilgerhaus on 07JAN08 and headed to Belvoir castle, the Jordan Valley. We had lunch at the Mount of Temptation restaurant. After dinner we proceeded to the Notre Dame center in Jerusalem, which was our home for the rest of the pilgrimage. The next day we prayed the Stations of the Cross at 5:30am on the Via Dolorosa and we celebrated Mass at Calvary. The Via Dolorosa is the traditional road that Jesus followed carrying the cross and 14 stations commemorate this. I had so many different feelings going through my mind as we prayed the stations. I felt a sense of awe knowing that our Lord went to the cross for our salvation.

17JAN08 We toured the Church of All Nations and the Garden of Gethsemane. A few days later we traveled to Beersheba, according to tradition, Beersheba is the place where Abraham binded Isaac and also dug a well there. The following week of 26JAN08 we visited Mt. Nebo, the place where Moses looked out and saw the promise land. The next day we visited Petra. Petra is one of the new Seven Wonders of the World. It has rock cut architecture and the large rocks are very beautiful. According to Arab tradition, Petra is the place where Moses struck a rock with his staff to bring forth water. Our tour guide informed us that we are only seeing nine percent of Petra because ninety-one percent of it is still buried in the sand.

We spent the night in Jordan at a place called the Jordanian. It is a very upscale place. It has a swimming pool, a Jacuzzi, fitness center, and you can see the Dead Sea out back. It is such a wonderful place and I wish we could have stayed another night. When we left Jordan and returned to Jerusalem we continued with our class work.

30JAN08 - I woke up and looked out of my window and it was snowing and it snow is rare in Jerusalem. Our scheduled tour of the city of David and the Western Wall was cancelled because of the snow. I spent the day reading the scriptures and catching up on my class readings. When February 1st arrived I was so excited because that meant that we were eleven days from returning home. I thoroughly enjoyed the pilgrimage, but I was ready to return home, so much so that I began singing Bruce Springsteen's song, "I was born in the USA."

Later on in the day we visited the Lithostrotos Convent of the sisters of Zion. We visited the Shroud exhibit at the Notre Dame center and afterwards we had some delicious fish and potatoes for dinner. The next day we visited Bethany and we celebrated Mass at Gethsemane. We also visited the site of Lazarus' tomb.

The following day we heard a talk from Catholic Relief Services (CRS) about the work that they do. Catholic Relief Services were founded in 1943. It is an international humanitarian agency of the Catholic Church in the United States that provides relief in emergency situations, and provides relief for millions of people throughout the world. For example, CRS responded to the 2010 earthquake in Haiti by embarking on a $200 million five-year relief and construction program that covers shelter and health. The presentation was very informative. CRS does amazing things such as working to strengthen the capacity for local communities to take control of their own development and CRS is dedicated to world peace. After the talk we visited Hebron to visit a few places where Catholic Relief Services is working. We visited a youth center in Hebron and a group of young people spoke to us about their frustrations regarding the Israeli and Palestinian conflict. Their stories were moving and powerful!

The next day I completed my assignment for our class on Ecumenism and completed my exams. Later on we visited École Biblique, a French academic institution in Jerusalem. The school specializes in archaeology and biblical exegesis and because of the wealth of information that we received I was reminded of the need to always pray and study the scriptures so that I can grow and be an effective priest for the people of God. Fr. Peter Damian Akpunonu told us that the primary duty of the priest is to proclaim the word of God. I will always remember this when I prepare to give my homilies. 11FEB08 arrived; we packed our bags and headed back to Chicago.

The Israeli/Palestinian conflict is very disturbing to me. It is such a complex situation that appears to have taken on a life of its own, and it is a powerful reminder of the need to proclaim the gospel message of faith, hope, and love. When I returned to Mundelein I finished the third quarter and spent the summer in New York in a Clinical Pastoral Education program at the VA hospital.

The Transition

I was ordained as a transitional deacon on All Saints' Day, November 1st 2009 by His Eminence Francis Cardinal George, OM.I. at Mundelein seminary in the Chapel of the Immaculate conception. It was a nice fall evening and several family members and friends came to Mundelein for the ordination. Here is the first sermon that I preached as a deacon:

Sermon

God's ways are not our ways. God's justice is different from human justice. (Isaiah 55:8) In today's gospel the parables of the laborers in the vineyard we see the difference between God's understanding of justice and our own. As you may know Jesus often spoke in parables to give us a glimpse of the unknown by illustrating what is known. In other words a parable means that one thing is understood in comparison with another. In this parable the known is the vineyard. The unknown is the reign of God.

The vineyard reflects one of the most common agricultural settings in first century Palestine during the time of Jesus. It was a large property and when the grapes were ready to be gathered the owner needed to hire additional workers to get the job done quickly while the fruit was in prime condition. The life of a day laborer was such that even a little pay might buy food so his family could eat for a day. The parable relates that the first group of workers agrees to the normal day's wage, those hired in the third, sixth, and ninth hour agree to whatever is right. Everything appears to be normal up until this point.

However, there is no mention of the payment for those hired in the eleventh hour. And the surprise comes by the action of the owner due to the order of payment. Normally those who had already worked twelve hours would be the first to receive their wages. But the landowner told the manger to begin payment with the last hired and end with the first hired paying each worker the agreed-on daily wage.

When the first hired came to receive their wages they assumed that they would receive more, but when they realized that they had received the same payment as those who were hired last they began to grumble. Now I believe that we can understand why those hired first would be angry, for they had labored through the heat of the day. Surely they would expect to receive more than those who worked less, especially more than those who only worked an hour. And it was certainly not common practice for a landowner to pay a full days wage for only an hour of work, but it is precisely here where we find the point of the parable. God's generosity is equally present to those who are called last. *God's ways are not our ways. God's justice is different from human justice.*

The reaction of those workers who worked through the heat of the day has to be taken seriously. We all know some people who would have practically killed the landowner for working long hours and getting the same pay as someone who worked an hour. They would have had some strong words for the landowner calling him every foul name in the book. But the message of Jesus says that there is a balance between God's justice and God's mercy. The workers who were hired first received a fair wage and a just reward. The fact that the workers of the 11th hour received the same wage displays the mercy of God.

My dear sisters and brothers in Christ, what began as an act of kindness to those hired first turned into an act of kindness to those hired in the 11th hour. The first group of workers did not see the generosity of the owner nor could they rejoice in the good fortune of their fellow workers who arrived late. *God's ways are not our ways. God's justice is different from human justice.*

The scripture says the earth is the Lords and the fullness thereof. ((Psalm 24:1) God gives to all who are willing to receive. Jesus teaches us that the goal of sharing is not more to those who do more or less to those who do less, but justice! When our justice begins to reflect the justice of God our entire human needs will be met. God shares with us because God loves us. The laborers of the 11th hour represent those who acquired the knowledge of Christ at the latest time. The laborers of the first hour represent those who have known Christ first, and the wages represent the Kingdom of God.

It does not matter when the Lord calls you, but when he calls you better answer. The scripture says that God's Spirit blows where it wills. (John 3:8) No one can monopolize the Spirit of God. The workers who grumble against the landowner are representative of those who are "too righteous" and want to play 'God' They say, "you have made them equal to us". (Matthew 20:12) How many of us draw up such superficial boundaries in order to distinguish ourselves from others? God does not care about how you look, or what's in your bank account. God cares about your heart. God wants us to show our love for one another.

The workers hired first are jealous of the good fortune of the other workers and they forget that it is the kindness of the landowner, which allowed them to receive any payment at all, and again the payment that they received was what they had agreed to. *God's ways are not our ways. God's justice is different from human justice.*

I stopped by here to tell you that God's justice is not about tit for tat, where you scratch my back and I'll scratch yours. God's justice is generous. God intervenes on the behalf of those that some would consider being outside the realm of God's love. The landowner was generous to all of the workers because he understood their needs Jesus ends the parable by saying the first shall be last and the last shall be first. (Matthew 20:16) When the first are last and the last are first everyone receives his or her just do. Jesus wants us to understand that we are all equal in the sight of God. God's ways are not our ways. God's justice is different from human justice.

God is supreme mercy and supreme justice. God's justice forgives the unpayable debts and it brings about peace. The scripture says the name of the Lord is a strong tower and the just person runs to it and is safe. (Proverbs 18:10) We are called to be united with the Lord and we all have a purpose in this life. But only you can discern your call. Some are called to the ministry, but that is only one way to serve the Lord. The scripture say that the Lord could make the stones preach if he wanted to. (Luke 19:40)

There is a calling to be a teacher, doctor, nurse, lawyer, engineer, policeman, fireman and countless others. Some are called to work with their hands like our Lord and Savior Jesus Christ to be craftsmen and builders, beauticians and barbers. Your call does not have to be related to an occupation. There is the high calling of marriage and the rearing of children, yes it is a blessing for wisdom to speak to youth. The scripture says keep your father's commandment, and forsake not your mother's teaching. Bind them on your heart always; tie them around your neck. When you walk they will lead you; when you lie down they will watch over you; and when you awake they will talk with you. (Proverbs 6:20-23)

So whatever it is that God calls you to do it is imperative that you answer the call, even if it is in the 11th hour. *God's ways are not our ways. God's justice is different from human justice.* **End of Sermon**

Hope for the Hood

As a police officer I had an unsettling view of a criminal justice system that in my view, takes for granted the poor and minorities, and on the other hand I witnessed the way in which some African-American youth contribute to their own demise. Initially, the things that I saw on the street were very fascinating to me, but as time progressed I began to internalize the things that occurred while working as a police officer. I became cynical and did not attend Church on a regular basis. The violence that I witnessed angered me at first, but then I just found ways to cope.

One of the most frustrating thing for me as an African-American man is to watch young men walk around with their pants sagging. It is my contention that this reflects the sad condition of some of our communities. This manner of dress says to the world that these young men have lost all hope and aspiration. When our youth decide to use and sell drugs I would argue that they have given up on life. When they join gangs and contribute to violence, instead of joining a church or any organization that seeks to make them better, makes me wonder if they are crying out for help. When our youth refuse to get an education they refuse to give themselves a chance in life. When young girls are having babies before they even know who they are, let's me know that we are faced with a spiritual crisis.

The ironic part of it all is that many of these young people are the very ones who have the potential to cure Cancer and AIDS. Some of them have the mental and rhetorical ability, when harnessed correctly to stand up and argue in front of the Supreme Court. But there is a disconnect, I don't want to point the finger at our youth who are lost, because there are other factors that play a role in the condition that they find themselves in. It can be argued that the educational system in the inner city is not up to par. Many jobs have been outsourced, and some in our community have grown up in dysfunctional families; it is like a vicious cycle that won't end.

We are living in a state of emergency. We have more young African-American men studying in prison as opposed to college. Violence continues to ravage our neighborhoods, but there is a way to break this cycle of violence. How? We must embrace the Word of God and hold ourselves accountable. We must fight all forms of injustice, whether it is violence, racism, sexism, war, poverty or economic injustice. One of the many things that I love about the Roman Catholic Church is her teaching on the Dignity of the Human person.

> "The dignity of the human person is rooted in his creation in the image and likeness of God (*article 1*); it is fulfilled in his vocation to divine beatitude (*article 2*). It is essential to a human being freely to direct himself to this fulfillment (*article 3*). By his deliberate actions (*article 4*), the human person does, or does not, conform to the good promised by God and attested by moral conscience (*article 5*). Human beings make their own contribution to their interior growth; they make their whole sentient and spiritual lives into means of this growth (*article 6*). With the help of grace they grow in virtue (*article 7*), avoid sin, and if they sin they entrust themselves as did the prodigal son[1] to the mercy of our Father in heaven (*article 8*). In this way they attain to the perfection of charity" (CCC 1700).

When we embrace our dignity as human beings we are able to reach our full potential in life and then we are able to work towards making the world that we live in a much better place. In order for us to be whole we must put God first in our lives and then become who God has called us to be. Human dignity means that we have the freedom and ability to shape our lives. We have the capacity for love and friendship that will allow us to transform our communities for the better. When we love our neighbor we recognize the dignity of the human person and we respect the rights and basic needs of others.

The Bible says that "God created man in his own image, in the image of God he created him, male and female he created them." (Gen. 1:27) The Roman Catholic Church is clear when she says, "Of all the visible creatures only man is able to know and love his creator. He is the only creature on earth that God has willed for its own sake, and he alone is called to share, by knowledge and love, in God's own life. It was for this end that he was created, and this is the fundamental reason for his dignity." (CCC 356) As human beings we are uniquely created in the image of God and so this man that we are called to do wonderful things with our lives.

In "*The Ethics of Authenticity*, Taylor states, "If the youth really don't care for causes that transcend the self, what can you say to them?" (Taylor, 19) I challenge our youth to put God first in their lives and to find out their calling in life. I had to find mine.

Chapter 12

Planting the seed

The Beginning

I was born in Chicago, Illinois on September 30th, 1966. My parents raised my sisters and I in Woodlawn on the Southside of town. Woodlawn was the home of the Blackstone Rangers. I was walking home from Mount Carmel High School One day when I saw a huge gang fight on 63rd and Stony Island. I would later find out that one of the Stones had been shot.

There was always trouble brewing in Woodlawn. I was walking to the store and all of a sudden I saw a man push down the Holsum bread man take his money and then shoot him in the leg. I could not believe this was happening. The man looked at me and then ran off. The storeowner came outside and helped the man. He told him that he had called the ambulance. The ambulance arrived and the bread man who was shot was able to tell them what happened.

I remember walking home from Mc Donald's with my food and then all of a sudden this guy comes from behind and snatches the bag right out of my hand. I chased after him but he ran into an abandoned building and I just chalked my food up as a lost.

My Father, Andrew Smith Sr. is a strong man and outstanding father. He was a part of Fr. George Clements youth group at St. Dorothy's when he was a teenager. Father George Clements was ordained in 1957 and was the second African American priest ordained for the Archdiocese of Chicago. He baptized me at Holy Angels in 1977. My faith journey began at Holy Angels as I began to learn about Jesus Christ. Fr. Clements is an excellent priest. He devoted his time and energy to preaching the Good News and promoting social justice. I can remember one Sunday that he asked all of the students to bring in their toy guns so that we can all throw them away. He was teaching us at an early age that there is no place in the world for violence. In his view, playing with toy guns was just a glorification of the violence that exists in the world.

I remember when my sisters and I would return home from school there were always at least four or five of our friends from the public school who would be waiting for us at the bus stop. As soon as we got off the bus wearing our brown uniforms they were there waiting for us making the sign of the cross, singing "Holy Angels, Holy Angels". I still laugh whenever I think about it. We transferred to St. Thomas during my sixth grade year. Some of the friends that I met there are still my friends today. I had a wonderful experience at St. Thomas. I was confirmed in 1980.

I graduated from St. Thomas the Apostle Grammar School in 1980. Our class song was "Hold On To Your Dreams", the words to the song our powerful and true, the author says, "dreams are the wings of the mind you can fly anytime you like." It is so important for us to believe in ourselves. God has given us such great gifts, but it is imperative that we use them.

I attended Mount Carmel High School. Our motto is, "You came to Carmel as a boy, if you care to work hard and struggle, you will leave as a man." The Carmelite priests were passionate about their faith and I assert that the religion classes that they taught were very practical. When I was a freshman, the bell rang and we were headed for our next class. I observed Fr. Wilda grab a star football player and throw him against the locker and say, "Don't you ever disrespect my class again." I thought to myself, how in the world I am going to make it through this dudes class next year. What I didn't know was that Fr. Wilda cared about the students. He was passionate about teaching and preaching the good news of Jesus Christ.

Fr. Thomas Wilda taught the sophomore religion class and he was able to make the connection between the gospel and the lives of the people. Fr. Wilda was an excellent teacher. I have asked several priest about him and they told me that he left the priesthood. Nevertheless, the scripture says, "You are a priest forever according to the order of Melchizedek." (Hebrews 7:17)

I'll never forget the day he came to class and gave the class stickers that had the word Apartheid on them. He instructed us to place them on the Stop signs. (Stop Apartheid) He was passionate about Jesus Christ and the gospel. In his view, liberation was at the heart of the Gospel.

Fr. Mike O'Keefe was the sophomore baseball coach. One of the things that I enjoyed about Mount Carmel was the competition in the Catholic league. There is a rich history of competition and for the most part there has always been a friendly rivalry between the schools. I enjoyed competing against Brother Rice, Leo, Hales, Mendel, De LaSalle, St. Ignatius and St. Rita because I had friends who attended those schools. I can remember one time when we were going to play Luther South, one of the coaches jokingly said, "Make sure you beat them because Luther quit on us."

We were playing St. Francis De Sales on a cold spring afternoon and I struck out looking at my first at bat. Fr. O'Keefe approached me as I went back to the bench and said, "Smith, I know that it is cold out here, but you have to adjust to the situation. If you don't swing the bat I will get somebody else who will." I borrowed a pair of my teammates batting gloves for my next at back and I hit a line drive single between the first and second baseman. Fr. O'Keefe is right, in life you have to adjust to the situation because we are not always faced with ideal situations, but we must make the best of what we have.

Dodging the Bullet

When I was a junior at Mount Carmel I didn't have any idea of what college that I wanted to attend. I was just an average student and mediocre athlete so I didn't have any schools beating down my door requesting my presence at their institutions. I was thinking to myself what am I going to do when I graduate from Mount Carmel? I came up with the bright idea of joining the Marine Corps. I notified a recruiter and he came to my house to speak with my mother, my father was at work at the time.

The recruiter came in and my mother greeted him told him that he could take a seat at the table. He was looking mighty sharp and intimidating in his dress blues. After he sat down he began to explain to my mother and I about what it takes to be a Marine. He said, "The Marines are dedicated to our country. The Marines are fearless." He then asked me to name some of the qualities that I have and he could tell me if I would be a good Marine. I said that I am courageous and strong. He said, "Well that's a major part of being a Marine." Nevertheless, my heart was beating real fast. I did not really want to be a Marine; I was just exploring some options. He was a true gentleman and very professional. He gave his presentation and then took out a pen and gave it to my mother so she could sign for me to off to basic training upon graduation.

I don't know what it was but I didn't have the heart to tell my mother that I didn't want to be a Marine. It seemed like forever when he requested my mother to sign the papers. I didn't look at him or my mother. I just stared at the table with my heart pounding away. The next thing I heard was my mother saying, "You can come back when he is 18 and he can sign for himself." I cannot begin to tell you the joy that I felt. My heart had settled down but I never looked up. I was somewhere between Lord have mercy and thank you Jesus! Nevertheless, I am ever grateful for our courageous men and women who serve in the military.

The Dream

A few months would pass by and during one of our class sessions on colleges and universities I read an advertisement in one of the college magazines that read Niles College is a place for dreamers. I thought to myself, this would be a nice place for me to go and study.

Fr. Clements, Fr. Wilda and Fr. O'Keefe inspired me, which led me to discern my call to the priesthood. I graduated from Mount Carmel in 1984 and enrolled in Niles College of Loyola University, the undergraduate seminary of the Archdiocese of Chicago. During my time at Niles I began to become more involved in the Church. After my first year of studies I spent the summer at St. Sabina as a part of the formation program. I was involved with the food pantry, which helped to feed the needy people in the community. I was involved in the summer program that included tutoring and athletic games. I enjoyed the experience of living and working at St. Sabina because it allowed me to put my faith into action.

As I matriculated through Niles College, my faith life began to deepen. I enjoyed many of my classes, but one in particular was, "The principles of Full Christian living." Fr. Sheridan taught this class. Fr. Sheridan instructed us in the cardinal and theological virtues telling us that the cardinal virtues will help us along life's journey. The cardinal virtues are **prudence, justice, fortitude**, and **temperance**. As I look back on my life I know that Fr. Sheridan was right. If we make these virtues a part of our life we will be able to flourish. The theological virtues are **faith, hope**, and **love** and they are the character qualities associated with salvation. Faith is such an important part of my life. My faith has helped me to endure some difficult times and it has inspired me to become a Roman Catholic priest. Hope is the key to a bright future. As a police officer, I witnessed so many youth who did not care if they lived or died.

I would argue that this is because they have lost hope. I believe that these youth have not been enlightened with the knowledge of God. We must pass on the faith to our children.

The Bruhs

During the summer and early fall of 1987 I pledged the Omega Psi Phi fraternity. The four cardinal principles of Omega Psi Phi are **Manhood**, **Scholarship**, **Perseverance** and **Uplift**. These principles are what attracted me to the fraternity because in my view these are foundational principles, and when you embrace them you are able to achieve many things in this life. After my first semester of what should have been my last year I had to withdraw from school because my grades were low due to the fact that I was doing more partying than studying. I did not at that time uphold our principle of scholarship. I remember one fall evening as I was working on a philosophy paper, the telephone rang and it was my fraternity brother. He said "I am on my way to pick you up; we are going to party with the Delta's at Northwestern University." I couldn't resist. Needless to say I failed that Philosophy class and I would eventually have to repeat the course in order to graduate.

I was having so much fun that I was not able to balance my time. I went on a road trip to the University of Illinois in Champaign Urbana and stayed with my fraternity brothers for a few days. I returned to Niles and spoke to Fr. McLaughlin. I told him that I was withdrawing from school because I was not doing well in my studies. Fr. McLaughlin was a very nice man and an excellent priest. He said that he was willing to work some things out with me so that I did not have to withdraw from school. Nevertheless, my mind and heart was just not in it.

I took a job working for the Chicago Transit Authority as a bus operator in 1987. It was a good job, but I knew that this would be temporary until I was able to get myself back into school. I met some wonderful people during my short tenure as a bus operator. Initially, I thought to myself, how can I drive this big bus? But I needed the work and so that thought faded fast. Driving the bus turned out to be the easy part. The most difficult part of the job was dealing with the people. I resigned from the Chicago Transit Authority in 1989 and returned to school in the fall. I still had the four cardinal principles of Omega Psi Phi (Manhood, Scholarship, Perseverance, and Uplift) in my mind, which gave me the motivation to return to school. These principles are in my mind and heart today.

I graduated from Loyola University in 1990. I had taken the police exam in 1989 in the hopes of being a police officer after graduating from college. However, I did not hear from the police department for a while and after graduation I was looking for a job. I was unemployed for five months and I was starting to feel a little nervous. I picked up the bible and read the Sermon on the Mount. (Matthew 5-7) I was immediately struck by the words, "Therefore I tell you, do not worry about your life, what you will eat or what you will drink or about your body, what you will wear. Is not life more than food and the body more than clothing? (Mt. 6:25) After reading these passages from scripture I was filled with a sense of deep peace. Shortly thereafter I found a job working as a substance abuse counselor for Interventions. I worked there until I received the call from the Chicago Police Department to take my physical. When I passed my physical, which was extremely extensive I began training at the police academy and I joined the Chicago Police Department in 1991, a job that I held until 2001.

Reflections of an Ex-Cop

I enjoyed my job as one of *Chicago's finest*. I met a great deal of wonderful men and women who serve the city with such distinction. There are a few officers who through racial profiling, corruption, and abuse give the majority of police officers who do a great job a bad reputation. I compare it to the priests who have abused children, although the abuse by priest is much worse. There is absolutely no excuse for this, for they have harmed human beings and betrayed the trust of the people of God. However, there are many priests who labor in the vineyard day in and day out, faithfully proclaiming God's word.

Sometimes officers are wrongly accused of using excessive force because some people believe that the officer is not allowed to use necessary force to make an arrest. I believe that most police officers would not be angry if they completed their tour of duty without having to wrestle with an offender.

Police officers and priests have some things in common. Both are called to provide service to the people. Police officers and priests often deal with people during crisis situations in their lives. Police officers and priests are people that you can trust, but again due to the horrible actions of some officers and priests the public perception is sometimes less than favorable, and this is understandable. Police officers and Priests are held to a higher standard because we are people of service. Again, most police officers and priests serve the people with pride and dignity.

The Ontological Change

I was ordained to the priesthood on May 23rd 2009, by His Eminence Francis Cardinal George, O.M.I. Archbishop of Chicago at St. Rita's Chapel. As I was sitting in the pews at the beginning of the ordination Mass I was overwhelmed with emotions. I fought back the tears as I thought about my long road to the priesthood. I was filled with joy and I could only say, "Thank you Lord!"

I was blessed to celebrate my first Mass on my mother's birthday the very next day, May 24th, 2009. When I was praying and studying to celebrate my first Mass, I wanted to deliver a homily that was faithful to the gospel and spoke to my journey and this is what the Holy Spirit inspired me to write:

Homily from my first Mass

My dear sisters and brothers in Christ, it is a pleasure to be with you here today as we give glory and honor to God. I am thankful to be able to celebrate my first mass here at St. Ailbe among my family and friends. My family has always stood by me and supported me and my friends have made me a better man. The African proverb says I am because we are and because we are I am.

And for those of you who don't know me, please permit me to introduce myself. My name is Andrew Charles Smith Jr. I hail from the Southside of Chicago. (Woodlawn) I was baptized at Holy Angels, and confirmed at St. Thomas the Apostle. I graduated from Mount Carmel High School in 1984. I submit to you that it was during these formative years that the seed was planted and I thought about becoming a priest. I attended the undergraduate seminary, Nile College of Loyola University and I learned many valuable lessons there.

Nevertheless, it was not my time. I was still trying to figure out this thing called life. I graduated from Loyola University in 1990, and shortly thereafter I joined the Chicago Police Department and worked as a patrolman for ten years. I really enjoyed many aspects of the job. I met many wonderful men and women who serve the City of Chicago with dignity, honor, and respect. Nevertheless, I was always troubled with the apathy that exists in many of our communities. It is disheartening to see the drugs, gang violence, and hopelessness that some people in our communities have succumbed to. These are few of the reasons why I said to myself that it is imperative for me to proclaim the message of Christ.

I was still not ready to become a priest because I wanted to marry and have a family someday. And so I gave some thought of becoming a protestant minister because they can get married. And so I did my research of theological schools and came across Candler School of Theology at Emory University. I resigned from the police department and headed south for the ATL to attend Emory University. Ironically it was at Emory when I began to grow in my knowledge and understanding of our rich Catholic heritage. I was able to view the Church in comparison to other religious traditions, and I came to fully appreciate our ancient tradition and powerful liturgy.

And working on the streets of Chicago where there is so much violence, I was struck by the Church's teaching on the dignity of the human person. In my view, this speaks to the contemporary issues of our time and it echoes the message of Jesus Christ. The Church teaches that the human person is the clearest reflection of God's presence in the world; all of the Church's work in pursuit of both justice and peace is designed to protect and promote the dignity of every person. For each person not only reflects God, but is the expression of God's creative work and the meaning of Christ's redemptive ministry.

When I was studying at Emory University I contemplated becoming a priest, but I struggled with the idea because as you all know the Church has gone through some rough times as of late. And when I was thinking about going to the seminary, the sexual abuse crisis was at its height. The sexual abuse crisis is a shameful and dark hour for the Church. It is a horrible sin and a down right embarrassment for the people of God. I pray for the victims and their families. St. Augustine said that the world is marred by sin. It is imperative be a reflection of God's love and justice on earth.

Despite this tragedy, I was able to see the true beauty of the Church. I know countless women and men of goodwill who have served the Church throughout the ages and I remember the words of scripture, you are Peter, and upon this rock I will build my Church and the gates of hell shall not prevail against it! (Matthew 16:18) And so after I graduated from Emory I was off to study for the priesthood and by the GRACE of God I am here. I remain humbly before you today, not as a model of perfection, because I have my flaws. Nevertheless, I stand boldly before you because I bear witness to the Divine guidance and perfection of the Father, to the eternal Word and Truth of the Son, and to the magnanimous and sustaining power of the Holy Spirit!

My journey to the priesthood has been filled with ups and downs, but I want to thank all of you who have supported me along the way. My family and friends have been there for me. The Knights of Columbus have been very generous in their financial support of all seminarians. The truth of the matter is that we are not always self-sufficient but dependent upon others, are family and friends, and always in need of God's grace, mercy and ever abounding love. Yes, the road to the priesthood has been long and hard, and there were days when I felt like giving up. Oh, but the scripture says, the man who puts his hand to the plow and looks back is not fit for the Kingdom of God! (Luke 9:62)

As I began my journey I heard all kind of things said about me. Some were good and some were not so kind. Some have questioned my integrity, and to those I can only lift up my sincerity. Some have questioned my morality, and to those I say I have fallen short of the glory of God, but I continue to press on toward the mark. Some have questioned my manhood. How dare they? The nerve of them, the audacity, the unmitigated gall! I am the son of Andrew Charles Smith Sr. When I was a little boy, my father and mother said son, your name Andrew means manly, and your middle name Charles means man. My nickname is man!

And yet others have questioned my sanity. They say how could you leave the police department to try to become a priest? Oh I stopped by here to tell you, the Lord called me. And the Lord's call transcends human status, (1Cor 1:26) it exceeds human strength, (1Cor. 1:25) and it confounds human wisdom! (1Cor. 1:18) The Lord's call is not based on the accumulation of worldly goods that will wear out like a garment and moth will eat away. There are treasures in heaven where moth will never destroy. (Matthew 6:20)

You see the Lord's call does not come from human beings; the Lord's call does not rely on human wisdom, nor is it fancied by human rhetoric, but by the preaching of the Cross! (1Cor. 1:17) This is why the Apostle Paul says that he wants to know nothing but Christ crucified. (1Cor. 2:2) Paul is not being unreasonable. Paul is not being unrealistic, the Apostle Paul knows the TRUTH! The apostle Paul knows in the depths of his soul that there is no knowledge superior to the love of Jesus Christ. Jesus Christ has shaken up the world and stripped Satan of his principal power. My sisters and brothers do not let fear paralyze you. We are all called and it is

141 of The Pulpit

imperative that we answer the call. Because when the Lord calls you better answer.

Today we celebrate the feat of the Ascension. The feast of the Ascension reminds us that we are living in a time between times. We are living in a moment of time where we have left one place in our journey but not arrived at the second. It is the already and the not yet. It is a time of tension. The already is God's victory over sin and death made manifest in the resurrection and ascension of Jesus. The not yet is the future. It is the coming establishment of the full reign of God's kingdom. We live in the midst of Christ's departure and return, but in the mean time what are we to do? In today's gospel we find the answer. Jesus commands his disciples and us to go into the whole world and proclaim the gospel to every creature. (Matthew 28:19)

The scripture says whoever believes and is baptized will be saved. And whoever does not believe will be condemned. (Mark 16:6) The faithful disciple is one that lives alert and active, following the commands of Jesus while awaiting the second coming and the consummation of the age. The Apostle Paul says we have to live dutifully and appropriately in this in between time. Yes, many of us are searching for peace of mind while living in a world filled with pain.

The Ascension of Jesus reminds us that we are only passing through this life. We are like Pilgrims on a journey. Just as Jesus' earthly life was temporary and came to an end, and he ascended into heaven to sit at the right hand of the Father, so also our lives will come to an end and we will meet God in the next life. The Ascension of Jesus makes us pause and consider, so that we don not forget what life is all about. The scripture says may God our Father enlighten the eyes of your mind so that you can see what hope his call has for you. (Ephesians 1:18)

It is already because in the Lord's hands our depths of the earth, the heights and mountains are his also. (Psalm 95:4) The Lord is robed in majesty and girded in strength, but it's the not yet because many of us are still paralyzed by fear. The scripture says that the Lord did not give us a Spirit of fear, but one of power, love, and self-discipline. (2Tim. 1:7) It is the already because in the Lord's name we have a power to expel demons, speak new languages, and lay hands on the sick so they will recover. (Mark 16:17-18) Nevertheless, my sisters and brothers it is the not yet because some of us refuse to tap into our God given potential and have bowed down to the false god's of materialism and immediate gratification.

But it's the already because the Lord has lifted up the first African-American president in a country that once espoused the spurious documents of slavery and segregation. We still have a great deal of work to do. We are living in a state of emergency. Violence continues to ravage our neighborhood. Many of our schools are failing and we have too many brothers in jail. We must take personal responsibility of our lives, and we must hold each other accountable.

When did it become fashionable for someone to walk out of the house with his or her pants sagging? Yes, I say her because I have even seen some sisters walking the streets with their pants hanging to the ground. I submit to you that this is ridiculous and downright ignorant. For this is not merely a question of style, fashion, or apparel, because this manner of dress tells the world that their hopes and aspirations have also dropped. We must demand more of ourselves because the Lord calls us to do extraordinary things.

My sisters and brothers in this in between time I pray in the words of the Apostle Paul: That Christ will dwell in our hearts through faith and that we will remain rooted and grounded in love so that we may have the power to understand with all the saints what is the breadth, and length, and height, and depth, and to know the love of Christ which surpasses all knowledge and that we may be filled with the fullness of God. As we celebrate the feast of the Ascension let us march on in faith knowing that we cannot live by bread alone, but by every word that comes forth from the mouth of God. (Matthew 4:4)

End of Sermon

Christ's peace,
Fr. Drew

Epilogue

I sit here on a fall, rainy day in Chicago. As I pen these words I reflect on my journey to the Priesthood. This book stands as a testimony to the power of God. God can transform anyone's life regardless of the situation.

Works Cited

Balthasar, Hans Urs von. *Razing the bastions: on the church in this age*. San Francisco: Communio Books :, 1993. Print.

Cabie, Robert. *History of the Mass*. Portland: Pastoral Press, 1992. Print.

Catholic Church, United States. *Catechism of the Catholic Church*. New York: Galilee Trade; Gift edition, 1995. Print.

Cooper, John. *Plato Five Dialogues*. second edition ed. Indianapolis: Hackett Publishing, 2002. Print.

Davis, Cyprian. *Black Catholics*. New York: Crossroads, 1995. Print.

Dulles, Avery. The assurance of things hoped for: a theology of Christian faith. New York: Oxford University Press, 1994. Print.

Flannery, Austin. *The basic sixteen documents: Vatican Council II; constitutions, decrees, declarations*. A completley revised translation in inclusive language. ed. Northport, NY: Costello, 1996. Print.

George, Francis E. *The difference God makes: a Catholic vision of faith, communion, and culture*. New York: Crossroad Pub. Co., 2009. Print.

Grube, G. M. A. *Five dialogues*. Indianapolis: Hackett, 1981. Print.

Hemesath, Caroline. *From slave to priest: a biography of the Rev. Augustine Tolton*. Chicago: Franciscan Herald Press, 1973. Print.

Johannes Baptist, Metz. *Poverty of Spirit*. New York: Paulist Press, 1968. Print.

Kant, Immanuel, Paul Guyer, and Allen W. Wood. *The Cambridge edition of the works of Immanuel Kant*. Cambridge: Cambridge University Press, 1992. Print.

Raboteau, Albert J. *A fire in the bones: reflections on African-American religious history*. Boston: Beacon Press, 1995. Print.

Raboteau, Albert J. *A fire in the bones: reflections on African-American religious history*. Boston: Beacon Press, 1995. Print.

Smith, Luther E.. Howard Thurman: the mystic as prophet. Washington, D.C.: University Press Of America, 1981. Print.

Taylor, Charles. *The Ethics of Authenticity*. Cambridge: Harvard University Press, 1991. Print.

Thurman, Howard. *Jesusandthedisinherited*. New York: Abingdon-Cokesbury Press, 1949. Print.

Thurman, Howard. *The creative encounter; an interpretation of religion and the social witness*. [1st ed. New York: Harper, 1954. Print.

Thurman, Howard. *Disciplines of the spirit*. [1st ed. New York: Harper & Row, 1963. Print.